THE GALAXY BRITAIN BUILT

The British Talent Behind Star Wars

By David Whiteley

Foreword By Robert Watts: Star Wars
Production Supervisor And Producer

The Galaxy Britain Built
© 2019. David Whiteley. All rights reserved.

No part of this book may be reproduced in any form or by any means, electronic, mechanical, digital, photocopying or recording, except for the inclusion in a review, without permission in writing from the publisher.

Published in the USA by:
BearManor Media
4700 Millenia Blvd.
Suite 175 PMB 90497
Orlando, FL 32839
www.bearmanormedia.com

Printed in the United States of America
ISBN   978-1-62933-498-1 (paperback)
         978-1-62933-499-8 (hardback)

Book and cover design by Darlene Swanson • www.van-garde.com

Dedicated to the memory of
Gary Kurtz and John Mollo.

Special thanks to:
Robert Watts, Les Dilley, Nick Maley,
Roger Christian, Peter Beale, Gareth Edwards,
Colin Goudie and Louise Mollo.

Also, thanks to Matt Wildash, Leslie Dilley,
Sue Rummery and Steve Knibbs.

Love and support from Amelia, Annabel and Cleo.

And to George Lucas, the maker, thank you and
May The Force Be With You, Always.

Contents

	Foreword	vii
	Preface	ix
Chapter One	Before the Empire	1
Chapter Two	On British Soil – Pre-production	13
Chapter Three	Getting High! – Pre-production	25
Chapter Four	Cameras Roll – Production Gets Underway	35
Chapter Five	On Set – Elstree Studios	43
Chapter Six	On Set – Elstree Studios: the Dark Times and the Light	53
Chapter Seven	Everyone Held Their Breath	63
Chapter Eight	At the Oscars and Elstree Strikes Back	97
Chapter Nine	The Force is Strong with the Next Generation	111
Chapter Ten	Monsters and Going Rogue	127
Chapter Eleven	The First Spin-Off	143
Chapter Twelve	The British Force	159
	About the Author	173

Foreword

by Star Wars Production Supervisor Robert Watts

I FIRST MET David Whiteley on a dreary October day, outside my favourite studio, Elstree, in North London. David greeted my assistant and me with a cheery smile and was bristling with enthusiasm to get me inside the studio and get the interview underway. He'd been in touch a few weeks earlier to say he wanted to document the work of the behind-the-scenes talent who'd helped make the original *Star Wars*. Then he tells me he was born on May the Fourth, 1977! I couldn't believe it. What a *Star Wars* birthday! So, a fan of the film, who was also making a documentary about it. Something struck me that this wasn't going to be a quick little interview and I was right.

David spent ages chatting with me, with two cameras rolling, under the lights in what was my second home as a filmmaker, Elstree Studios, sound stage number 8. It felt like he left no stone unturned. I was telling stories I'd never told before and his face lit up as he tried to maintain a professional air of a documentary maker, but the *Star Wars* fan in him just couldn't help himself.

This was just the beginning and for me it felt as if I had travelled back in time, to the happy days of being on set with all the cast and crew.

It brought back wonderful memories of working with such talented people, who were all brought together by George Lucas.

George led me into a world that completely changed my life and, to be fair, completely changed cinema forever.

This book has brought together the memories of some of the British talent who I had the honour of working with on *Star Wars*.

David's love of the movie and determination to help record the stories that underpin this piece of cinematic history are most impressive!

I thought I'd heard everything about the making of *Star Wars*, after all, I was there! But then I read this book....

Robert Watts

Preface

"The Adventures of George Lucas"

A LONG TIME ago, in Los Angeles, California, a young movie director was hawking a script around; film studio after film studio. The script had a clunky title to say the least: "The Adventures of Luke Starkiller as taken from the Journey of the Whills, (Saga 1) The Star Wars." And if any studio executive made it past the opening page, they were bombarded with a far-fetched story, filled with odd character names and comic book dialogue. Worst of all, it was science fiction. No one in Hollywood was interested in making a science fiction movie. The box office for the genre was dead.

It was frustrating for the man behind this seemingly doomed project. George Lucas was "the darling of Hollywood" at the time. As a young director he'd enjoyed success making the now cult movie *American Graffiti*. Universal had financed that picture but, for reasons best known to the executives at the time, they were not interested in backing his science fiction idea. In fact every major Hollywood studio passed on the project. Everyone... except 20th Century Fox.

But the schedule was tight and the budget even tighter. It soon became obvious that shooting in Hollywood was going to be far too expensive. The cheaper option: Britain. And, as they say, necessity is the mother of invention! Those British filmmaking 'inventors,' creators and designers would play a vital role in bringing George Lucas's movie to life. Most self-respecting *Star Wars* fans know of the struggle. But this is the story of how the biggest movie of all time, the movie that would define a genre and a generation was very much, almost by accident, a British endeavor. Here it is, told in the words of the people who made it.

This is 'The Galaxy Britain Built....'

CHAPTER ONE

Before the Empire

(From interviews with
Producer: Gary Kurtz
20th Century Fox Executive: Peter Beale
Production Supervisor: Robert Watts
Set Decorator: Roger Christian)

STAR WARS IS very much part of our modern-day culture. It's everywhere. So it's very tricky to picture a time before then. But, of course, there was.

In the 1970s, it was all about taking risks. Studios wanted young, edgy directors, who would dare to be different. In 1973, George Lucas made a name for himself, with *American Graffiti*. His right-hand man, Producer Gary Kurtz, recalls just how little money it was made with.

> "It was such a low budget film. We made it for eight-hundred and fifty thousand dollars, shot it in twenty-five days, so we expected it would at least make its money back!"
>
> – *Gary Kurtz*

Well it did much better than that. It took one hundred and forty million dollars at the box office for Universal. Lucas and Kurtz suddenly had the attention of the industry. A young film-making duo, who could turn a few hundred thousand dollars into a hit film! Surely, whatever idea they pitched next would be snapped up, right?

George had his space opera script, the one with the clunky title, and, along with Gary, they were taking it from studio to studio.

> *"The science fiction films that were released in the seventies, tended to be rather dour, post-apocalyptic stories, which were very depressing. We wanted 'Star Wars' to be a Flash Gordon-type space opera which was an adventure story, exciting but with enough humour and lightness that it would be an enjoyable experience, especially for the kids."*
>
> *– Gary Kurtz*

But despite their enthusiasm, Hollywood was reluctant to bite.

> *"The film was turned down, a lot, because science fiction was not very popular in the seventies at all and it was quite arduous in a way to be turned down, but that was very common too."*
>
> *– Gary Kurtz*

However, the success of *American Graffiti* had caught the eye of an executive at 20th Century Fox. A name synonymous with the history of *Star Wars*: Alan Ladd Jr. Gary Kurtz remembers how they got a foot in the door.

"Alan Ladd Jr. saw a copy of 'American Graffiti' before it was released in the cinema and said, 'Well this is a good film'."

– Gary Kurtz

A good film and one made on a tight budget. So maybe this could help persuade them that *Star Wars* was worth a gamble.

"He did have some trouble convincing the Board of Directors, though, and I have to admit that the script was not easy to read, because it was full of odd names and funny descriptions. We had no visuals to show at that time, so it was a leap of faith on their part."

– Gary Kurtz

20th Century Fox agreed to back George Lucas and take a chance on the movie. But they would keep a very close eye on the production. Peter Beale was a young executive working for 20th Century Fox in London. He'd worked his way up through the ranks and his previous experience on a Hollywood movie made him an ideal candidate to assist with this exciting science fiction project. As Peter Beale recalls, they'd managed to make a big movie on a tight budget before.

"We got a script called 'The Omen' and Warner Brothers had turned it down because it was going to cost three million dollars and Alan Ladd Jr. said, 'If you can make it for two point eight million, we'll make it.' And so that was my first job and I brought together a crew and worked out how to make it."

– Peter Beale

So, Fox made *The Omen* but Peter Beale's magic with film finances was about to be put to the test.

> *"A script arrived and I read it and I was very surprised. George Lucas had made 'American Graffiti'. He was the darling of Hollywood. Universal had financed it, so why weren't Universal going to finance this film? And Alan Ladd Jr, or Laddy as we called him, said, 'Well not only has Universal turned it down, but Warners and everybody else has.' I realised there must be major problems, because if the experts of the industry had turned it down, I actually thought it would be impossible to make."*
>
> – Peter Beale

In the meantime, Alan Ladd Jr. had convinced the 20th Century Fox Board to take a chance on George Lucas. He needed an answer from his British-based exec, Peter Beale.

> *"Laddy said, 'Can you make it?' I said, 'I don't know, but let me find out. I need a month.'"*
>
> – Peter Beale

George Lucas and Producer Gary Kurtz had the tentative green light. That was good enough for them. But Gary says it would be a while before they saw any money.

> *"After they said yes, we worked to figure out a proper budget and production plan. We were spending our own money for the development period."*
>
> – Gary Kurtz

As part of the production plan, Gary needed to get everything in place. The priority was to find a space big enough to film in, a task easier said than done.

> "Well, originally when Fox gave us the go-ahead, I was assuming we were shooting at Fox in L.A. Of all the other pictures I've made before that, even studio financed pictures, they were all shot on location. So, it wasn't until I went in there and spoke to the production people that I realised that was going to be a problem because they only had two or three stages available. We needed at least seven. They trawled around town and said we can get you two at Universal, maybe two at MGM and I realised, logistically, that that was a nightmare. They were scattered all over Los Angeles and it was not a good idea. And then someone in the production department said, 'Well, talk to our office in London, the Fox office, they may have some suggestions about shooting in Europe.' So, I travelled around Europe, I went to Paris, I went to Rome, I went to Budapest, I went to Berlin, I went everywhere where there was a film studio and the only other place to have the space was one in Rome. But that had been downplayed for me by several other American filmmakers; they said it's too noisy. The Italians don't know how to stay quiet for live sound, so, we knew we had to use live sound, so I came back to London."
>
> – Gary Kurtz

Once in London together, Producer Gary Kurtz, Director George Lucas and the Executive in Charge of Production, Peter Beale, got their heads together. Peter remembers the script was fantastically ambitious.

> *"There were incredible logistics, special effects, models and other things, problems that needed to be solved. So I first of all have to make sure they could be solved and then that it could be done for a reasonable amount of money. And then George, Gary Kurtz and I sat down and we went through the script line by line. And we agreed: George made some suggestions and I made suggestions and we came up with the final formula of how we were going to make it."*
>
> *– Peter Beale*

By this time, it was pretty much established that *Star Wars* would be shot in Britain. The deal, sealed by Fox's man in London. Peter Beale had analysed the whole production and told his bosses in L.A. it could be made for half the price tag of filming it in Hollywood. The initial budget was four million dollars.

It was now time to assemble the top tier of the behind-the-scenes talent who would help bring the galaxy to life. The stunning concept art, which had helped to sell the story to 20th Century Fox, was the work of Ralph McQuarrie, in the U.S. And the special effects department was to break new ground in California. But it looked as though a significant part of the force, behind the Force, would be the Brits.

Producer Gary Kurtz needed someone he could trust to supervise the ambitious production.

> *"I had met Robert Watts at MGM and I asked him if he would be interested in being the production supervisor on the picture; he had a good background and a good reputation."*
>
> *– Gary Kurtz*

Robert Watts, who'd previously worked with Stanley Kubrick, remembers the very moment the phone rang.

> *"Well, the first time I got the call, I got a call from Peter Beale who was then the head of 20th Century Fox in London and I was actually out in Greece, helping out on a film they were doing there and he said, 'Gary Kurtz is coming to England and he's asked to see you.' Well I'd met Gary some years earlier in L.A., when I came back from shooting a film in Mexico and I was at MGM studios. He came up to ask me what it was like filming in England, so I told him and I thought no more about it. So, dissolve! I flew back to England, met Gary Kurtz and then flew back to Greece and finished the job out there. And then I heard I'd got the job on 'Star Wars'! It was many years later that I really discovered why I'd got the job and I actually asked Gary. I said, 'How did I actually get the job Gary? Was it because I'd met you in L.A.?' He said, 'No, it was because Stanley Kubrick recommended you.' And I went: 'Oh wow!' Because by then Stanley was dead and I could no longer say thank you to him. But I had worked with him on '2001: A Space Odyssey'. So, in a sense, it was a science fiction film that led me into a science fiction film!"*
>
> *– Robert Watts*

As production supervisor, it was Robert's job to get things sorted, keep the wheels in motion and, above all, get the best deals possible. After all, the budget was tight and the location for filming could potentially drain a lot of resources. And Robert was after a LOT of sound stages!

"I went to Pinewood Studios and I said to the head of the studio there at the time, I said, 'I want to rent every single stage you've got in the studio.' And he said, 'We never rent every single stage to one production.' So I said, 'Alright then.' So, I went to Elstree Studios and went to see Andrew Mitchell, who ran the place, and I said, 'I'd like to rent the entire studio.' And he said, 'Be my guest.' And he gave me a deal of seventy-five thousand pounds for the entire studio, everything, all the stages, all the workshops, everything. Fantastic! It was the best deal I ever made in my life. I loved Andrew and he was a great studio manager to work with because he'd been a film producer as well, so he understood what we needed."

– Robert Watts

As Obi-Wan Kenobi famously says in *Star Wars*, 'In my experience there's no such thing as luck….' That may well be the case in that galaxy, far, far away for a certain wise old Jedi, but lady luck was certainly smiling on Robert Watts! It just so happened that a movie called *Lucky Lady*, starring Gene Hackman, Liza Minnelli and Burt Reynolds, was being shot in Mexico. That film was about to provide some of the crucial talent that was to make *Star Wars*. *Lucky Lady* had a team of British art directors on the production, but they needed more help. A world away from the dry, humid air of Baja, Mexico, the phone of Set Decorator Roger Christian was about to ring in a very wet and grey London.

"I remember finishing a movie. I was at home in West Hampstead, it was raining. The tennis at Wimbledon was on and they were thinking it was going to snow. And I'm

there thinking, 'Yeah I'd better get another job, really.' And the phone rang. And it was 20th Century Fox. They said, 'Are you interested in a film we are doing in Mexico? We have a team of British art guys out there. Les Dilley, Norman Reynolds and John Barry, they need help, this film has got huge.' And I said, 'When will it be?' He said, 'You'll have to leave Wednesday.' It was a no brainer. I said, 'Thank you very much.' I was on the plane, read the script on the plane on my way over and it was one of the best scripts I've ever read."

— Roger Christian

Lucky Lady, directed by Stanley Donen, was all about the Prohibition Era and smuggling liquor. The screenplay was written by friends of George Lucas: Gloria Katz and Willard Hyke. They'd also collaborated with George on the screenplay for *American Graffiti*. And they'd been talking with George about his vision for *Star Wars*. He wanted to create a very real galaxy, nothing plastic looking, like the science fiction films that had gone before. So, Gloria and Willard invited George and Gary Kurtz down to the set in Mexico.

"I went down to Mexico to Baja, where they were making 'Lucky Lady' and the writers on that project, were friends of ours, they were some of the writers on 'American Graffiti'. We talked with John Barry, who was the designer of 'Lucky Lady'. And he was making these amazing dusty western sets. They looked incredible."

— Gary Kurtz

Freshly hired Set Decorator Roger Christian distinctly remembers that very moment when George Lucas and Gary Kurtz arrived on location.

> *"I was dressing a salt factory, because it was a valuable commodity in those days, where it was unloaded and we had this old peeling front with faded lettering and I was shovelling this salt when a car arrived. Out got George in his plaid shirt, jeans and sneakers and Gary in a cowboy hat. They walked over to me and introduced themselves. George said, 'What are you doing? This is amazing, the look of this,' and I showed him, he hadn't realised it was fake. We'd built it on the front of an old building. And George helped me, he got a shovel and we were shovelling salt together. We got talking about science fiction. I said, 'I love science fiction and I really despair about the films that are being made so far. They think you have to have plastic guns that go 'beep' and the sets look completely unreal,' and I said, 'I see it like an old car that's dripping oil, and in a garage, that's being repaired.' And he said, 'That's what I'm making, that's what I want to do, I don't want anything to shine or be noticed.'*
>
> *– Roger Christian*

George Lucas wanted a 'worn-out' looking universe. Almost as if the audience was only dipping into this world, getting to see just a glimpse of what had gone before. And it appeared George had found common ground with the salt shovelling, British set decorator, as well as the rest of the British art department working on *Lucky Lady*. Roger says things were pretty much sorted over dinner.

> "We had dinner with George that night. Les Dilley was away on location but Norman Reynolds was there, John Barry and myself. We were talking about how it should look. With science fiction, there is nothing to go on. There's nothing to reference. George couldn't say, 'I want it like this,' he would just say, 'I want it like a dusty western, combined with 2001.' Which fortunately I understood, which is exactly what he wanted."
>
> – Roger Christian

And he wanted this team, this British team. Production Designer John Barry, Art Director Norman Reynolds, Assistant Art Director Les Dilley and Roger set decorating. But the gruelling schedule in Baja, Mexico took its toll on Roger and he says he barely made it out alive.

> "I was so busy working I got paratyphoid. I was dying, literally. I got to the point where I was about to die, in a clinic in Ymas. I was eight stone, I was so bad. We left and I went back to L.A. They sent me there to make sure they'd cured me. While I was still recovering, John Barry came back to see me and said, 'George has offered us this film, meet me at Alice's Restaurant,' which was in Malibu. So, we met for lunch and caught up and he said, 'If you want to set decorate the film, George has asked for you. You've just got to be back in England really soon.' And I said: 'I'm in, I'm doing it.'"
>
> – Roger Christian

CHAPTER TWO

On British Soil – Pre-production

(From interviews with
Assistant Art Director: Les Dilley
Production Supervisor: Robert Watts
Set Decorator: Roger Christian
Costume Designer: John Mollo)

THE BEHIND-THE-SCENES TALENT was coming together. But the deciding factor for Fox giving the green light was shooting it in Britain, because of the cost. It would be much cheaper in the UK. But the less money there was, the more creative the art department would have to be with the cash they had! As Roger Christian recalls:

> "We met there in London, they gave me an office by the canal. There was just John Barry, Les Dilley, myself and Robert Watts, that was it. And George and Gary. No one else at that stage. The second day we went to 20th Century Fox in London and met Peter Beale and he said, 'This is the budget for the movie. It's four million dollars.' Then I finally got a script. I broke it down; it took me ten days. I had a list of

weapons, robots, sets, vehicles. I just stared at it in horror thinking, 'I can't do this.' We sat in the office, John Barry and I, saying: 'How are we going to make this film? It's an epic!'"

— Roger Christian

Les Dilley, who had been an assistant art director with this team on *Lucky Lady*, felt very lucky himself to be working with them on this 'epic,' despite everyone's concerns about the budget. There was definitely a momentum gathering in this tiny London office as these young, creative minds got to work. It was awe-inspiring for Les.

"It was fantastic. I was working with Norman Reynolds. I'd been with him for a long time because I'd been learning from him on a TV series we'd worked on together. And here I was now, on 'Star Wars', with John Barry and Norman Reynolds, running the show. It was just incredible. So much talent in that room. And I'm standing there, thinking I'm mind boggled with all this talent and cleverness. Being able to draw, like they drew and sketch like they did and also have the knowledge of how to make it all work. That's what I was always really excited about, being a part of it. I never thought I would get into the art department, but I did."

— Les Dilley

George Lucas presented them with the initial concept art: six paintings by Ralph McQuarrie. From these designs, a whole new galaxy would have to be created. And a believable one at that. It had to feel genuine. And, as much as the art department had to bring that all to life, George was also after someone who could work from those drawings to create the costumes and characters from a galaxy, far, far away…. Peter Beale, from Fox, remembers he had some suggestions about who would be best suited to be the costume designer.

> *"George chose, but I recommended. Looking at the film, looking at the script, there were two elements to the costume design. One element was Princess Leia; clearly she had to look beautiful, so we had to have somebody that could do that. But that was one element amongst a hundred elements of Stormtroopers and Wookiees and a whole series of bizarre figures. A lot of which had a military-type theme. I worked with John Mollo on 'Doctor Zhivago', he was the technical consultant for Director David Lean for all the Communist aspects of the film. And I got on with him very well and he'd become a costume designer. And so I suggested him and one other person. And George chose John because of his military background. And it was a great decision. And when I saw his designs, I thought they were just fabulous. Better than I imagined. That's the great thing about the crew, you always wanted to do something better than you can imagine. And most of them did!"*
>
> *– Peter Beale*

John Mollo had started out as a military historian and advisor. Before *Star Wars*, John worked with Stanley Kubrick on the film *Barry Lyndon*. And it was John's attention to detail and knowledge of military uniform that George wanted to utilize. But this was John's first foray into science fiction.

> *"I'd never done anything like it before. But I found it was quite a straight-forward story, quite a comic story really. But*

> *I was working from concept art. Quite a lot of design work was done before in the United States."*
>
> *– John Mollo*

But from that concept art, the very modest John Mollo had to make those costumes come to life. Darth Vader, Stormtroopers, Han Solo, Princess Leia, Luke Skywalker, Chewbacca, the list seemed endless. John got to work, sketching in his workbooks, very much as he had done all his life, with military precision. Only this time, he was trying to interpret everything in George Lucas's mind, creating a world of make-believe, the likes of which no one had ever seen before. And in the early stages of pre-production, when George was going back and forth to the States, John would prepare his sketches and wait for the verdict.

> *"There were times when he was in America and that made it slightly more difficult. I mean all you could do was just prepare to show him things when he came. This was quite early on, just show them to him when he came back. We'd discuss things between us and it was a question of who won and who didn't win that particular day!"*
>
> *– John Mollo*

But John says there were very few disagreements over the costume designs.

> *"We never seriously disagreed, we were only talking about details really. The basic thing was fairly well settled."*
>
> *– John Mollo*

Throughout John Mollo's sketchbooks, as well as the evolution of iconic *Star Wars* designs, he was making countless notes, drawing on his years of historical military knowledge. All of this would prove invaluable to the look of *Star Wars*. Next to sketches he wrote Western and US Cavalry, or Nazi type uniforms. It was a huge project, but John took it all in his stride.

> *"It was quite a normal procedure, I did the same with other films. I would take my military knowledge of costume and uniform and change things. We were sort of assembling it all and improving what we thought needed improving to make the costumes unique. But the costumes were pretty simple on the whole."*
>
> *– John Mollo*

But things were not simple for the art department. John Barry, Norman Reynolds, Roger Christian and Les Dilley had their work cut out. Design the stuff, get it made and do it as cheaply as possible. But John Barry would come up with ingenious and cost-effective ways of solving problems.

> *"I had this idea of getting a lot of junk. We bought fifteen thousand pounds worth of wrecked aeroplanes and took it to pieces and used those pieces, which in themselves are very interesting. For instance, the bar where they meet Han Solo, the whole of the bar back is built of old jet engines, lacquered gold."*
>
> *– John Barry - BBC interview. 1978*

At Elstree Studios in Borehamwood, Set Decorator Roger Christian remembers when the lorry loads of junk started turning up.

> "Frank Bruton was the prop master in charge. He'd worked with David Lean, with Kubrick, everybody. He said to me, 'Boy,' he used to call me boy, 'what do you want boy, what do you want me to do?' I said, 'I need you to strip your prop room out, just strip it bare.' Then a sixteen-wheeler lorry backed in, piled with aeroplane jet engines, scrap, you name it. Frank Bruton's next to me, he didn't even look at me, he just said, 'You know you're mad, boy, don't you?' I thought, 'Yeah, I probably am.' Because we didn't know it would work."
>
> – Roger Christian

They then set about taking everything apart. The art department wanted anything and everything that looked interesting and, once deconstructed, would look nothing like its original purpose. After all, this all had to look like it existed in another universe, not the one we inhabit. And while the junk was being turned into bits and bobs for the vast *Star Wars* sets, Roger and Les Dilley had another joint project to sort out: R2-D2 and C-3PO.

> "The first thing Les and I got having read the script, R2-D2 and C-3PO are the story tellers. George took them from 'Forbidden Fortress', where there are two peasants, minor characters but they tell a story. George got this idea of these squabbling peasants, that was those two, right? We realised if he didn't have those characters, we didn't have a film. It couldn't be made. C-3PO we knew could be done, because of the 1927 movie 'Metropolis'. They got a fairly similar suit on an actor and we knew that with the right mime actor or dancer, he could be made. R2-D2, the scale that Ralph McQuarrie had drawn him and George's idea, he was three

foot eight, three foot nine, something like that. And radio control was very primitive in those days. It wasn't the best."

– Roger Christian

And because they couldn't rely on a remote control R2-D2, Roger was convinced they needed an actor to be inside the robot. That was the only way they could bring this essential character to life.

"We were pressuring George and Robert Watts to hire someone who could fit inside. Because we knew we had to work it, with a person inside it. It wasn't going to work otherwise."

– Roger Christian

And they had just the actor in mind. It fell to Assistant Art Director Les Dilley to get Kenny Baker to be the performer who would bring this droid to life.

"First of all, I had to persuade him to do the job. He was on 'Oppo Knocko'; well that was 'Opportunity Knocks' on TV, it was very, very popular. He and his sidekick had a band and they played music together and they were about to do it. He said, 'Well I don't know, I think I'm going to do 'Oppo Knocko.'' I said, 'Look, I tell you what. I think you should think about it seriously, because this is going to be a major film and it's probably going to make you famous.' And that's how I got him to come into the studio for an audition and he said, 'OK, I'll do it.' And then he said, 'What about my partner? What am I going to do? I'm splitting the partnership.' I said, 'Well there's some other parts he can play as well.' And in the end they both were in the film."

– Les Dilley

With Kenny onboard to play R2-D2, the team had to then start turning the concept art for the droid into a reality. Roger turned to an old friend and colleague in the film industry.

> *"I'd worked with a carpenter who'd done sets for me, Bill Harman. Bill's a kind of cheeky chappy, always laughing, never complained. Always playing jokes. He did all of the sets and special effects and props for 'Monty Python'; now they really had no money in those days. Their budgets were like eight-hundred thousand dollars. So we hired Bill, John Barry took him on, and we had to make R2-D2. I looked at Bill and he said, 'Well I've asked Robert Watts, he won't give us any money, they don't have any.' He said, 'I've got some marine ply at home.' He brought the marine ply from the garage, because marine ply you can steam and bend it. So, we made a frame. He said, 'Well Rog, I can't make the top, I haven't got any money.' Lee studios were Lee Electrics, they were one of the big film lighting companies. I went round the back and asked where their scrapheap was, where they threw everything away and they showed me this pile of junk and I found this lamp top, from a rifle lamp from the 1940s and I thought that's the right size. So I didn't say anything because I knew if I'd gone in as a set decorator they'd ask me for quite a few pounds. So I said, 'Bill, go and buy it.' 'Alright Rog.' He got it for 10 shillings. He told Robert Watts recently, 'You know I still never got my ten bob back!'"*
>
> – Roger Christian

At every twist and turn of the movie, it came down to the budget. Production Supervisor Robert Watts had to spread the money very thinly!

> "20th Century Fox, who were financing the film, didn't believe in it at all and gave us a terrible hard time, because they didn't believe in it. Basically they didn't give us enough money to make it, they didn't give us a long enough schedule to shoot it in. We had the tightest schedule you could possibly imagine and the lowest budget you could possibly imagine. And it was a constant battle, day by day by day. And so everyday was a kind of battle."
>
> – Robert Watts

The behind-the-scenes talent had to continue to be very economical with their budgets. Using junk and bits and pieces, whatever they could find. It was a creative process, but hard work. Roger Christian put in endless days to get his vast list of props assembled before the cameras rolled.

> "We were working such ridiculous hours, it was seven days a week. We met in my office at seven every morning. I had a kettle, and McVities chocolate biscuits, which the film industry runs on. It was always John Barry, myself, Peter Dunlop the buyer, Frank Bruton, Les and Norman. We would need to get together early in the morning because we would often not speak throughout the day, because we were so busy trying to pull this epic together. And to be honest, if you had the conventional art department, everything was drawn, then went into the plaster shop, then the prop shop, and it was all made and built. We didn't have the money for that."
>
> – Roger Christian

The look of *Star Wars*, that is known and loved throughout the world, came out of necessity to make the sets and props with very little cash. The science fiction weapons were certainly no exception. Roger remembers trying to find something to arm the Stormtroopers with, at a place where he'd bought old weapons for other movies.

> *"I said 'do you know what, I've got to do Stormtroopers guns, what I think might work would be Sterling sub-machine-guns'. So they gave me one. They set me up with the table, my buyer had got me a roll of T-strip. So I stuck the T-strip around the barrel, which gave it a really cool look. Then I said 'have you got anything like gun sights?' They pointed me in the back. I found a box of army night sights. The army had used it in Ireland, you could look through and see at night. I really liked the shape of them so I stuck that on the top. And then I said, 'You know the clip, it's too big, it doesn't work.' They said, 'We've got one that fires three shots, just a little short one.' I stuck that on and I thought, 'Wow this is quite a cool weapon!' And it could fire. It could do single shot, multiple shot, so you got the flame and the smoke. And then I thought, from my list, Han Solo. George has always described him as a Western hero. So I said, 'Let me look at your pistols, what you've got.' I said, 'Is there anything like a modern Western?' And they gave me the Mauser, which had a wooden handle. I love the look of it. I said, 'That's the one.' So I got a silencer from a different gun, stuck it on the front. Stuck the biggest sight on the top of it and I thought: 'Wow these are quite cool!' And they look used."*
>
> *– Roger Christian*

Then, the moment of truth. Roger felt like he was taking a chance, but he had to get approval.

> *"So I made a call to John Barry at the studios and I said 'you'd better bring George over here and look at what I'm doing.' And I thought this is it. This is the moment where I'll be fired, or I'm on the right track. So George came. He just took one look. And what he liked was the actors could fire the thing, the guns would fire. So he stayed with me and we made Princess Leia's gun. It was a practice pistol. I thought the shape was good so George stuck with me. So I said, 'I want to show you something while you're here.' Because Ralph McQuarrie had painted Chewbacca with like an assault rifle. And I'd seen this crossbow, which had balls on the end, which I loved. So I said, 'George, I want to show you something, maybe it would work for Chewbacca.' And he just smiled and embraced it. We changed Chewbacca from that moment. And I said, 'I'll add on some sights and make it look more like a gun than a crossbow.' That's still the one he uses to this day. So, I was on the right track with George!"*
> *– Roger Christian*

The arsenal for the galaxy was taking shape, thanks to Roger's ingenuity and his interpretation of George Lucas's concepts for *Star Wars*. The young set decorator was building a good working relationship with George. But the biggest test of all lay ahead: To find the weapon that would not only define a character, but become one of the most iconic movie props of all time.

"I hadn't tackled that; the lightsaber. We called it the laser sword because we were British! I knew this lightsaber was the Excalibur of this film, I knew it would be the iconic image. It was amazing! But I couldn't find that, anywhere. So I went to Brunnings on Great Marlborough Street in London, whom we rented all our film equipment from: photography, anything we needed, and I'd buy equipment there. I just said to the owner, 'Do you have anything here that's unusual, or stuff that might be interesting?' He pointed me over to the side of the room. He said, 'There's a load of boxes under there, I haven't looked at those for years, go and have a rummage through.' And it was the first box, it literally was covered in dust. It hadn't been out for, I don't know, fifteen or twenty years. I pulled it out, opened the lid and there was tissue paper and then when I pulled it open, now it goes into slow motion… out came a Graflex handle from a 1940s press camera. I just took it and I went 'There it is! This is the Holy Grail.' And there were about five or six in there, we bought the lot. I raced back to the studios. Got my T-strip, stuck that round the handle, I stuck seven round it. From a calculator I'd been breaking down there was a bubble strip, where the light illuminated the numbers and they would magnify and it just fitted into the clips, so I just cut it, stuck that in. Called George over again. I said, 'I think I've found the lightsaber George.' He came over. It was heavy; he just looked at it and smiled. That's the biggest approval you can get from George, he just smiled."

– Roger Christian

CHAPTER THREE

Getting High! – Pre-production

(From interviews with
20th Century Fox Executive: Peter Beale
Creature Maker: Nick Maley
Producer: Gary Kurtz
Assistant Art Director: Les Dilley
Production Supervisor: Robert Watts)

WHILE THE ART department tried to bring the sets and props to life, there was another team trying to populate this imaginative galaxy that George Lucas was creating. When Production Supervisor Robert Watts struck the deal to shoot the movie at Elstree, his stupendous deal of seventy-five grand didn't just include all the sound stages, it was for all of the buildings on the site. One of them would become home to the make-up department. Now make-up on some movies means just that, but not on this one! Stuart Freeborn was in charge of creating the creatures that would inhabit the make-believe galaxy. Peter Beale, who was heading up the London office for 20th Century Fox, remembers when Stuart was brought onto the production.

"Make-up, it's so important, especially on this film. If you look at it, there's a lot of it you don't see. Stuart Freeborn started doing make-up before the Second World War. I was privileged to work with him; he was the first suggestion, the only suggestion, and of course he was fantastic. And he brings with him a great crew and he knows how to manage them."

– Peter Beale

Nick Maley was one of his crew. He had been plugging away at a career in the film industry for a long time.

"I worked with Stu Freeborn in 1971 on 'Young Winston', a movie about Winston Churchill when he was young, but I hadn't done a creature effects movie with him so I was really on tenterhooks."

– Nick Maley

It had always been Nick's dream to work in films.

"I was fortunate that my dad was an actor. We were a pretty poor family, living in a council house in Kingsbury, just on the outskirts of London. But my dad managed to live his life the way he wanted to, as an actor he did shows in the West End and he did the ice shows at Wembley, he sang at the end of the pier in the summer. So he lived his life the way that he wanted to. And that, I think, is a great success. For me, he helped me understand that it was possible to live life not within the confines that everybody else expects, to grow up and have to take a job that you don't really want to do, just to pay the bills. And I decided, I didn't want to sit in

an office and I didn't want to work in a factory. My dad had worked as one of the foreground performers on 'Oliver' and so he knew a couple of guys, make-up artists. I'd learnt make-up as a kid and then I knew this is what I wanted to do. Make-up in the movies!"

– Nick Maley

But getting to where Nick wanted to be, working on major movies, like *Star Wars*, would take a lot of hard graft and involve some setbacks too.

"I worked on a version of 'Julius Caesar', with Charlton Heston, as Mark Anthony and John Gielgud and Diana Rigg, and all kinds of big stars. That was very exciting! I thought, 'I've arrived! Here I am, I'm on the set.' And then after a few weeks they didn't need me anymore, and I was like, 'Here I am, I am unemployed!' That's the nature of trying to do something difficult and that's actually the time when a lot of people give up. But it did drive me on further but often people will say, 'I'm trying to do it but I'm not making any money but I have to take an extra job.' I drove a laundry van for a while. Because I could be finished by midday and be by the phone at three o'clock, when they were calling people to go and work on movies. You have to do what you have to do to get through. I had a period when I had no money apart from two months' rent and I paid one month and that gave me eight weeks before I was going to run out of money. I kept the second months' rent. I didn't have any money for food. I'd show up at my friends' houses at meal times and they took pity on me and said, 'Would you

like to share some? We were just going to have something to eat.' They didn't know that I'd shown up deliberately to try to get some food. Fortunately, after six weeks, I got a film job and I was able to pay the rent and get some food."

– *Nick Maley*

Nick Maley was persistent and, because he'd worked with Stuart Freeborn before, he gave him a chance on *Star Wars*.

"I was the new kid on the block. I got all the rotten jobs! There were only six of us in this room, the old schoolroom, at Elstree Studios."

– *Nick Maley*

It was the early days of the creature workshop. They were working from the concept art to bring the weird and wonderful to life. But, like the rest of the production, they didn't have much money, or indeed, time. As Nick recalls.

"We were starting at eight in the morning and finishing at eleven at night and we were sitting in this little room. And every night Paul McCartney's band 'Wings' were rehearsing 'Venus in Mars' on the big soundstage so we had all of this great music coming through while we were trying to get this stuff done. It is a great memory. There were five or six of us working in there and on one side were the mixers, where we made the foam latex, which filled the room with ammonia, and on the other side we were painting with toluene paint. But we had all the windows closed because it was cold. Looking back, we were probably all high at the time!"

– *Nick Maley*

And Nick says he had to grin and bear the jobs he was given!

"I started out by making eyes for all the UK creatures. You'll see they walk around, they don't have irises, or eyeballs, they have kind of a glossy eye that was actually made by blowing lighting gels into shape with an air compressor, but we did that outside and it was cold out there and no one wanted to go out there. I got that job. But eventually I took over doing the foam runs and it was extraordinary. Stu (Freeborn) was just maybe two metres from me, he was building Chewbacca. So, when he needed a third hand I would go over and mix the material or hold something steady for him."

— *Nick Maley*

In the 1970s, the team that was making the moulds just had to get them fabricated as quickly as possible. Of course, all of the *Star Wars* creatures and characters have names. But back then, Nick says they made up their own names for them.

"The characters, such as Dr Estavan, at the time these guys were ugly, one through five. Greedo wasn't Greedo, he was one of the five Martians, and we called them Martians. They got their names changed afterwards. Crocker, one through three, or Bat Alien! The only one that had the name that stuck was Snaggletooth, and that was because someone came in, after he'd been sculpted, and said, 'Oh, he's a funny snaggleytooth, isn't he?' And that name stuck! I was really doing a lot of the groundwork. It was a great learning curve for me because I learnt how to do all the foam latex work. I was watching how other people were working. For me the critical thing was the networking. The networking is the most

> *important part of getting to a point where you are working frequently. We were all freelance people. And that was an essential part of why we ended up being all-rounders. We were doing sculpting and we were making moulds and we were building puppets. We just couldn't find anyone else who could do the job. At the time there were other movies being made. Those people who had worked with Stu on other movies were busy doing other things. And so that was just the way that it was!"*
>
> *– Nick Maley*

The whole team, working on creature production, worked long and hard to get the aliens made in time for filming to begin. Nick says the man in charge, Stu Freeborn, expected results.

> *"Stu was a very cautious guy. He was actually a hard taskmaster, he expected a certain standard and he ran the place like a headmaster, so we were kind of cautious to make sure that we kept him happy."*
>
> *– Nick Maley*

Just working on a movie was very special for Nick. All he'd ever wanted was to be doing this, creating something special, alongside the greats of the industry. Stuart Freeborn was already a legend in the filmmaking world and for Nick to be part of his team was a dream come true, even if those employed on the film didn't quite understand what was going on.

> *"No one had a clue that 'Star Wars' was going to be 'Star Wars' until it became 'Star Wars'!! Right?! The script seemed a bit hokey, a bit boy's own really. We were just happy to be build-*

ing things, you know? Number one: we had money in our pockets, number two: we were doing fun stuff, rather than just making pretty girls look prettier! I'm not sure that any of us on the movie knew George Lucas. I mean, George was a young, thirty-something guy, in a baseball cap, sitting over by the camera. We were impressed to be working with Alec Guinness and Peter Cushing and 'It's directed by who? George who?' but he was the 'Governor' so we all respected him that way."

–Nick Maley

As pre-production progressed, the British behind-the-scenes talent was certainly impressing the American bosses. Producer Gary Kurtz remembers the diligence of the British team on the movie.

"I think they brought a level of professionalism and kind of hard work that I hadn't seen in Hollywood immediately before that. Hollywood got, I thought at least with the crews I worked with, a bit slack, especially on TV. They were making TV movies, some of which I worked on, where you probably only had ten days to shoot an hour and a half film. It was really difficult; you were working thirty to forty set ups a day. Coming to the UK and working with a British crew had a fairly organised system, we were able to accomplish what George wanted on the set. They worked very hard. Even if they were sceptical about whether the film would be any good or not, they certainly put the effort into it. And I have to say, the art department really came into their own on 'Star Wars'."

– Gary Kurtz

But, apart from a handful working on the film, Gary recalls there were many who found the story hard to grasp!

> *"I think most of the crew thought it was a silly film. They didn't get to read the whole script and so there were some humorous scenes in it. Several of the crew thought it was more like a 'Carry On' film rather than a serious science fiction film. It wasn't either, actually! It was a light space fantasy, which was a term most people had not heard of, so they weren't sure how it was going to turn out."*
>
> *– Gary Kurtz*

Assistant Art Director Les Dilley was working as diligently as the rest of them and fully behind George Lucas and Producer Gary Kurtz, even though there were those around him who weren't sure the film would appeal to audiences.

> *"I don't think we really understood it. And I do remember a couple of people on the crew saying, 'Well, what is it? A load of rubbish, what does all this mean?' They really said things like that. And, of course, at the end of it there were apologies coming from these people and I won't mention their names. There were two or three who thought it was a load of rubbish and what we were doing. They had to literally make a personal apology for saying what they said."*
>
> *– Les Dilley*

Certainly, as production got underway, the 20th Century Fox Executive in Charge, Peter Beale, remembers those reservations all too well.

> "I think initially there was a certain scepticism that it was a bit of a comic book. Remember that special effects movies, space movies, had not been successful, except '2001'. And '2001', which of course was made in England, was sort of a kind at the intellectual end. So, really, space and special effects were considered sort of B movies. And this was a comic book, expensive B movie, I think a lot of people thought. But I think as they got into it and they started to understand it, and when they looked into the Force and all that aspect of it, which was so important, they started to understand the difference."
>
> – Peter Beale

There may have been scepticism from some of the crew over the film, but from the art department and many of the other Brits working on the movie, George Lucas had tremendous support. And anyway, despite any reservations, there was no turning back now. The costumes, creatures, props and sets were ready to go and the actual production was about to get underway. And for the director, the producer and the production supervisor, the headaches were really about to begin. In charge of supervising the production, Robert Watts knew his first challenge was Tunisia: the real world location for far away planet, Tatooine.

> "To start with I was dead scared because I wasn't sure what was going to happen. We were starting shooting the film in Tunisia, in North Africa, and I thought, 'If I can get through this bit in Tunisia, if I can get this done, get out of here and back to the studio, I think we should be alright.'"
>
> – Robert Watts

CHAPTER FOUR

Cameras Roll – Production Gets Underway

(From interviews with
Set Decorator: Roger Christian
Assistant Art Director: Les Dilley
Producer: Gary Kurtz)

THIS WAS IT. Principal photography was imminent on George Lucas's space opera. Tunisia in North Africa had been selected as the perfect location. It would be the backdrop for what we now know as some of the most iconic scenes in *Star Wars*. R2-D2 and C-3PO would crash land here. It was Luke Skywalker's home. It's where audiences would first meet Han Solo and his trusty, hairy best friend and sidekick, Chewbacca. And it was also where the Jedi Knight, Obi-Wan Kenobi, was living in self-imposed exile.

But, according to Set Decorator Roger Christian, Obi-Wan Kenobi should have been living in much more opulent surroundings. But, yet again, the budget put paid to that, and maybe for the better.

"The original drawings Production Designer John Barry did from the script, Obi-Wan Kenobi had a huge cave complex. That ended up becoming one room, to save money. In the end I think destiny struck again, because he's a simple kind of Buddhist and mentor, so he shouldn't have a whole complex. That was right."

– *Roger Christian*

The midnight oil had definitely been burned - and then some! Many of the production crew, those in the art department, and the creature workshop, had put an incredible amount of hours in. Seven days a week, as Roger vividly remembers.

"We prepared this huge science fiction film in two and a half months. It was insane. Absolute madness. They had to start in Tunisia because everyone was worried about the weather getting too hot. The other thing was the Landspeeder, we thought how the hell are we going to make this thing? It had to look like it was floating in the desert and there wasn't CGI then. That didn't exist. My colleague Bill said, 'Well, I've got some wheelbarrow wheels at home.' So we got wheelbarrow wheels and some of his plywood and we built, with polystyrene, we built a Landspeeder. And then George said, 'You know what? A young kid would have a sports car, a beaten-up sports car. He wouldn't be able to afford one like that.' So we built three, one like a beaten-up sports car! Bill still says he remembers to this day as he was welding body bits on it, George Lucas was watching him, and he said, 'That's the worst bit of welding I've ever seen in my life'."

— *Roger Christian*

Camera Roll — Production Gets Underway

Worst bit of welding or not, it did the job, just about. Now there was yet another moment of truth, filming in Tunisia. *Star Wars* was in production. The tonnes of scrap and junk that the art department had been working with to make the sets cheaply had to be transported all the way to North Africa. And that was Roger's responsibility.

> "I took jet engines down. They said, 'You're taking scrap to Tunisia?' and I said, 'I've been there, they don't have scrap. Everything is used. These worlds are not like here in the West.' And I looked at an aeroplane they had there, to see if we could use it. But they had confiscated one of Gaddafi's planes. And it was there, mothballed, but they said, 'You can't touch it. We've taken it, we've captured it from Gaddafi.' So, I had to take the truckload of scrap. They thought I was mad, it's like taking coals to Newcastle."
> – Roger Christian

Everything was shipped to Tunisia: the scrap, the costumes, and the sets. Lorry after lorry was loaded for the journey from Britain, the now home of the *Star Wars* production, to North Africa. Assistant Art Director Les Dilley says the problems really began for them in the desert.

> "We built all the stuff in the studio, shipped it all out. Six containers, forty-foot containers. We'd built it in the studio, put it all in the boxes, shipped it all to the desert. Now the homestead had a big disc on the far side, it was probably twenty-five or maybe thirty-foot diameter. It was very big. It was like a big dish and all the little lights round the side of it. There was a vertical, then a dome over the top. Two days

before shooting, this thing comes out and I go, 'That's where it sits, we've got a little wall round and it sits on the top,' and we plonk it on there and it's got all the electric lights working and it's all checked and it's beautiful, done. As a crew, we're all shaking hands, thinking how clever we all are. Off we go. Come the next morning, seven o'clock, we turn up. This dish has disappeared. It took about twenty people to pick it up, because it was so heavy. It was up and you couldn't see it. It had got up on its edge and it went probably half a mile. We couldn't see it. It had gone like a big wheel, flying down the road with the wind. The wind just got it and threw it down the road like it was a ping pong ball!"

– Les Dilley

OK, so they had problems with the set.... disappearing! But thankfully the cast was sticking around. And what a cast! There were three unknown actors: Harrison Ford, Carrie Fisher and Mark Hamill. But George Lucas had some British heavyweights onboard, including Peter Cushing and the biggest name to grace the *Star Wars* credits at the time: Sir Alec Guinness! Set Decorator Roger Christian was there when the legendary British actor performed his very first scene, as exiled Jedi Knight, Obi-Wan Kenobi.

"Alec Guinness arrived, I was there when he did his first shot. We were in the canyon, the famous 'Star Wars' canyon where he walks in, his first scene in the film, those were the first shots done. Before the take Alec went and rolled in the sand, on his own. Didn't ask anybody, just went and rolled in the sand, got himself all dusty and dirty. And then he did his take. That's a man dedicated to a vision and what he was

doing. And we were staying with Alec Guinness in the hotel, and his wife. Alec was incredibly professional, he was always there on set, on time. And I think of his stature, being on that film. I made this assumption afterwards, and I think it's true, that it gave George Lucas a credibility. The others were young upstart Americans, you know, which to Brits it was like, 'Oh they're not actors, they don't do Shakespeare, they're not really actors.' He was Alec Guinness, he was really the giant, with Laurence Olivier. I don't really know of any other actor who could've made those lines just resonate so powerfully as him."

— Roger Christian

While Sir Alec Guinness was giving his interstellar performance alongside the young Mark Hamill, as Luke Skywalker, there were two other characters that were integral to the *Star Wars* universe in Tunisia. The storytellers, the droids: C-3PO and R2-D2. For Producer Gary Kurtz they were certainly the trickiest things to get right!

"I think the robots were our biggest challenge because almost everything else was a logistical exercise, getting it done, but the robots were a part of the cast. Their personalities were important, their ability to move about was critical to shooting various scenes. We went out to Tunisia without ever having had the time for Tony Daniels, for instance, to wear the entire C-3PO suit. It was a real exercise then, especially with wind and sand blowing around, to get him into the suit and the movement that was required. We had to curtail some of the shots we wanted to get because it was really difficult for him. And with R2-D2 we had a radio control

unit, but it was very primitive radio control at that time. And it didn't work very well. We even had problems with the Tunisian Air Force when they would fly overhead. The radio signals from the aircraft would activate R2-D2 and he would wander off across the desert! But the biggest problem with Artoo in Tunisia was the mechanical effects people had worked out to convert from the two-legged version, which had Kenny Baker inside, and he operated everything manually. That was the easy version of Artoo, that worked fine. The radio control version didn't work so fine, but to convert from the two-legged to the three-legged, they had this one model that had an explosive bolt in it. It would fire the third leg and tilt the Artoo forward and it would fall onto that third leg so that it could roll forward. Well, most of the time it didn't work and just fell over."

– Gary Kurtz

R2-D2, a beloved character and hero of *Star Wars* now, was quite frankly a nightmare to bring to life in 1976. With no CGI and primitive remote control, Roger Christian says it was down to the creativity of those behind the scenes, to make sure Artoo would be able to perform when the cameras rolled.

"A few weeks before, John Barry called Les and I into the office and he said, 'I don't think the radio control robot is going to work. Build a lightweight R2-D2 that we can pull on fishing wire; take it with you, don't say anything just keep it in the truck. Take it down.' So, we did. We built one. The first day, the first thing on set with R2-D2, he crashed over! Les Dilley and I watched. And we got out our one. And laid

down a board, put sand against the edge of it and they could only shoot from a certain angle. Most of R2-D2 in Tunisia is shot with Kenny in it, or being pulled on our fishing wire. There are very few radio-controlled moments. George always said when he started shooting that he was getting sixty percent of what he imagined it should be."

— Roger Christian

Les Dilley remembers how Kenny Baker gave R2-D2 his cheeky personality, when they first started shooting in the scorching temperatures of the Tunisian desert.

"When he operated it, it was a bit like a human being. He rotated the head and he's tweeting the noise! Because he had the controls in there to turn the thing and the lights. The actual noises were put on afterwards. He did a great job! And for me it was just magic, being part of building R2-D2, and bringing him to life."

— Les Dilley

Filming in such conditions was gruelling for everyone involved. Les says it was movie making on a grand scale, with little budget.

"It was pretty ambitious and it was not easy to do. From where we were staying, we used to go out into the middle of nowhere and put all of the stuff together - and it was BIG stuff! All coming out of these giant containers. I was building bits and when you're building sets, often you're working six or seven days a week, to get it made in time!"

— Les Dilley

Set Decorator Roger Christian remembers all too well the very long drive between the two different production bases in Tunisia.

"We were going backwards and forwards between Tozeur and Djerba, it was a fourteen hour drive, it was hell for me. I was driving little rental cars. There were no phone communications. We had to phone London to get a phone call between each site. They felt sorry for me, so I had matching drawings in both hotel rooms. They were permanently there, because if there was a flood and I was called I would have to drive fourteen hours through the night because Les had to stay with the unit."

– Roger Christian

Eventually, the location shooting was complete. George Lucas had his Tatooine exteriors in the can. Producer Gary Kurtz says thanks to a crew who worked tirelessly in the desert.

"When I'd look at the daily reports and some of the footage, I'm amazed that we actually finished on time. But we did. The crew was really good. We were warned in advance the British crews were very sticky about the time of day they worked, but on location they were fantastic. We worked really hard, they would work really long hours and gave up Sundays to work. I can't praise them more! They were the main reason we were actually able to finish on time."

– Gary Kurtz

CHAPTER FIVE
On Set – Elstree Studios

(From interviews with
20th Century Fox Executive: Peter Beale
Production Supervisor: Robert Watts
Producer: Gary Kurtz
Set Decorator: Roger Christian)

THE CREW WAS back on British soil and it may have been hot in Tunisia but it was also a tad warm in London. It was the infamous heat wave of 1976. George Lucas was about to embark on the bulk of the shooting schedule. There had been challenges in North Africa, but they would pale into insignificance, compared to what was on the horizon. The Executive in Charge of Production for 20th Century Fox in London, Peter Beale, had to tackle one tricky little issue that arose from the actor's union.

> *"Equity was trying to look after the British actors, there was no work around and they didn't want foreign actors coming in and taking mid-size roles or big roles that the British actors could do, because there were some wonderful British*

actors. And so to get a permit for a foreign actor you had to go to the Home Office and apply. The Home Office would call up Equity and see how they felt. So you really had to go to Equity first! So, to get a work permit for Gregory Peck on 'The Omen' it was actually jolly difficult and it took a lot of negotiating skills to get it. When we came to 'Star Wars' and George said he wanted three unknown young actors from America to play the lead roles, it was going to be very, very difficult. But we fortunately had some wonderful parts for the British actors: Alec Guinness, Peter Cushing, Dave Prowse etc. etc. So what I did, and I'm not ashamed of doing it, is I created a cast list with Guinness and everybody else at the top. And at the bottom, in what looked like minor roles, Harrison Ford, Carrie Fisher and Mark Hamill. The three American people. And I went to Equity and said, 'Look, the British have got the best parts in this, but the director wants three little Americans for the smaller parts.' And I also went to the Home Office and told them the truth. And I said, 'This is what I'm trying to do' and they supported it because they wanted the work and they recognised it. And Equity, I don't know if they knew or not, but they finally agreed. And so the first cast list, which is somewhere knocking around, has these major actors at the bottom of it."

– Peter Beale

You'd think that Equity might be a little perturbed with Peter Beale's reworking of the cast list, to get the stars of the movie their permits, but once *Star Wars* came out, they soon forgave him!

"I think that they recognised at that point that the film had been successful and I had to go back to them on other films and they were always very friendly. And we were in talks about second films and stuff so by the time they realised I think they'd forgiven me."

– Peter Beale

So, with the official permits sorted, it was time for the sound stages of Elstree Studios, or EMI as it was known then, to become the interiors of the Millennium Falcon, the Mos Eisley Cantina and the Death Star. Even though the production supervisor, Robert Watts, had worked with Stanley Kubrick on *2001: A Space Odyssey*, he says the sets and the costumes were beyond anything he could have imagined.

"Well I started on 'Star Wars' in 1975, before any sets had been built and the rest of it. Then we started to make the movie and I went onto the sets and the sets were fantastic! John Barry, who was the designer, had done an extraordinary job, along with John Mollo the costume designer, of course, based on conceptual designs by a guy called Ralph McQuarrie, who's sadly not with us anymore. And it was weird, it was amazing. Darth Vader, Stormtroopers, all of that. It was something I'd never seen before; it was something that was new, it was exciting, it was different and, hey, I hoped it would be successful."

– Robert Watts

The young director, George Lucas, was shooting a movie in Britain for the first time. Robert Watts had built up a working relationship with him during pre-production and their time on location in Tunisia.

> *"George was coming to England for the first time and prior to making 'Star Wars', you know, he had not made big pictures. 'American Graffiti' for example had probably been the most important film he'd made up to that point. And Fox had intentionally, quite correctly, I don't knock them on that, got people in positions around George who had made big films, so that they could help him in adjusting to making a film of that size. Like John Barry the production designer and John Mollo the costume designer and me, the production manager, the rest of us had all done big films and we came in and worked with George. And I really liked working with him."*
>
> – Robert Watts

Just as with everything on *Star Wars*, money was the deciding factor in most decisions made for the movie. As Robert recalls:

> *"20th Century Fox, who were financing the film, didn't believe in it at all and gave us a terrible hard time, all the way through shooting. Basically they didn't give us enough money to make it. I don't think George had expectations when he came here. He was slightly forced to come here by 20th Century Fox because they wanted to make it for less money. But once George came here and he worked with British talent, actors and technicians, he realised what he'd got over here is, hey, I don't want boast but probably the best in the world."*
>
> –Robert Watts

On Set — Elstree Studios

The art department had been very busy, using the concept art, beautifully painted by Ralph McQuarrie, and turning it into a reality. Peter Beale recalls such skill from the British talent working on the movie.

> *"The art director does a lot more than art directing. He runs an enormous department, building complicated sets which are mechanical sets, civil engineering; it's a very, very important job. And it was a great team of art directors: Les, Norman and Roger."*
>
> *– Peter Beale*

And leading them: the highly talented production designer, John Barry. From their designs, they were now getting the galaxy built for George, under the watchful eye of Producer Gary Kurtz.

> *"We knew it would be a big construction build and John Barry was very keen on seeing what can be done to help speed the process up. So we used a lot of experimental techniques towards the end of the shoot. We used a vacuum-forming machine quite a bit and it was a new technology at the time. I think we bought the first one available in the UK for the production because it will allow you to stamp out all sections, for instance. You would make a mould of one out of plaster and you could then stamp it out on plastic and just tack it up on the wall. We used that for several sets because we had endless corridors on the Death Star, which were the same, rather than having to sculpt them all. So it was a great help."*
>
> *– Gary Kurtz*

The Death Star was, of course, where the heroes of the galaxy would almost meet their end, in the trash compactor. Set Decorator Roger Christian was now very well versed at working with junk, to get everything looking just right … and for the right price, of course!

> *"I had to do the garbage incinerator room in the Death Star. So we built that on the tank, it was full of water. I had to do scrap, that they could be in. So, I couldn't use the heavy stuff, they could get injured by it. And polystyrene was notorious, if you cut it. It would be white. I had my buyer buy every form of PVC drain piping. We had stacks of it. I had to make that rod that Harrison (Ford) holds. I could not do it and I found a junction piece and it was bending so I just went down to Harrison and I said, 'You've got to help me out Harrison, I can't get this to work.' He said, 'No, don't worry.' I showed him what I wanted. And he made it work as an actor. They were compatriots, because he had to hold it and it was bending. That thing would have fallen apart. I had to find a way to inject polystyrene and make lightweight stuff. That set drove me nuts!"*
>
> *– Roger Christian*

The sound stages at Elstree were a hive of activity. George Lucas was under tremendous pressure to stick to the schedule, which was tight. Peter Beale, who was the eyes for 20th Century Fox, says the production schedule in London, for the most part, kept on track. But they had to work within the tight hours, set by the unions.

> *"Always filming is difficult. It always is, as we would say 'a kick, bollock and scramble' to get things done. George was*

initially concerned because in those days we worked very rigid hours. The trade unions demanded that we didn't start until eight-thirty and we finished at five-thirty, and there was no flexibility. Except if you had started shooting before the lunch break you could take an extra fifteen minutes to finish a shot and if you had started shooting a shot before five-thirty, you were allowed an extra fifteen minutes to finish it. So to get the work done you had to be very disciplined. But that also allowed the film crew to have a life at home. It wasn't absolutely a bad thing. And the only way you could keep on schedule was by getting the first shot very quickly in the morning. So, you have to have a director who's prepared to come on the set, get the first shot, and a camera crew and a crew that understands that and gets moving. A film crew doesn't start until the camera starts rolling."

– Peter Beale

It's been well documented that George Lucas and Producer Gary Kurtz found this rigidity frustrating. This was a completely new way of working for Gary.

"In Hollywood, my experience had been that you can work overtime - you just pay for it, within the limits of course. They will do a certain amount of overtime if you need it, but here it was down to a system where, when five-thirty came if you wanted to work over, you stopped and you had a meeting with the shop stewards and they decided if it was OK to work over. And I could never quite figure out what that process was because I was never part of those meetings. Because some days everybody said 'Fine', other days 'No!' Yes it was

frustrating, especially for George, because if we were halfway through a scene and it would only take half an hour more, then we felt why would this be a problem? But that didn't happen all that often. Most of the days were planned pretty well and the crew worked fast. It was a minor annoyance."

– Gary Kurtz

They stuck to the filming hours, set by the unions. And although Gary Kurtz remembers it as a minor irritation, Peter Beale says it did create tension.

"George and Gary came to me and complained. And I explained that's the way it is and many fine directors: Fred Zinnemann, David Lean, etc. had managed to do it. And I'm sure he could manage. And he did."

– Peter Beale

Every time something went wrong, the production team would have to come up with solutions. It seemed on *Star Wars* this was happening frequently. But for Peter Beale, having worked on many major productions before *Star Wars*, this was all just part of the process.

"We had crises in the film, you always do. We had ours in the process work. We had worked out that we wanted to do the process where the actors were inside the spaceships with star backgrounds and the fighter backgrounds. We wanted to do that with a new front projection material, this was this 3M material. And Charlie Staffell had worked out how to do this. Now this was going to be important, because we would

be able to have on camera the first generation quality effect so the quality would've been much much better than if we had gone to what is called blue screen, where you photograph an actor against blue and after the film, you put the spaceships in behind. You lose generations. So, we had prepared for this. We're half way through the film, things are going quite well, and suddenly the background plates that were being produced in America didn't turn up."

– Peter Beale

Producer Gary Kurtz remembers they had to revert to the old way of doing things. But, as was proving very much the case with *Star Wars*, problems seemed to resolve into solutions that were ultimately better.

"ILM hadn't produced any of the plates. They were way behind and I had to change over to blue screen. So we used the front projection equipment to project a blue screen onto the background, and in a way it's a good thing we did because it meant we could match the timing of the images in the background in post-production. Better than we could while the actors are working on the stage. So in the long run it worked better that way. Any film is full of problems. You are solving a problem or hundreds of problems every single day. So you expect that, it's how you do it I suppose that's the answer. You can get overly frustrated. I know several filmmakers who'd gotten to the point of despair, because the film is not turning out the way they wanted and I don't think you can ever expect so. You are better off planning for the worst

possible circumstance, hoping for the best and always settling in the middle somewhere. You shouldn't get disheartened by it. It's very possible the end result could be better than you envisioned."

— Gary Kurtz

And, as the American producer discovered, the British tradition of popping to the pub after work for a pint, became central to coming up with those answers.

"George actually had a hard time in the UK personally, because he didn't like the weather much, or the food, and he hadn't been away from home a lot. He just wanted to get through the day's shooting and go home. The tradition of British crews is that you finish the day, you go to the pub, and there was always one in the studio. And you chat about the day and what you want to do the next day. It's part of the socialisation of this system. George didn't want to participate in that at all, so I did some of that. I'm not the most social person in the world, but I realised from a work point of view this was an important part of the day, the way the British system works. So we found it quite useful. We did discuss potential problems for the next day's shoot and sometimes solve them there in the pub."

— Gary Kurtz

CHAPTER SIX

On Set – Elstree Studios: the Dark Times and the Light

(From interviews with
Set Decorator: Roger Christian
Production Supervisor: Robert Watts
20th Century Fox Executive: Peter Beale)

As Britain sweltered in the excessive summer heat of '76, a beleaguered young American director continued his mission to get his space opera in the can. But he faced challenges on a daily basis, all the while balancing the set filming hours of the crew and the tight schedule, and even tighter budget. Set Decorator Roger Christian remembers it all taking its toll.

> "It put George in hospital. He collapsed with exhaustion and they thought he was having a heart attack. That was part of the pressures of this film!"
>
> – *Roger Christian*

George certainly had the backing of the art department and his production supervisor, Robert Watts. But Robert recalls tensions between George and the director of photography on the picture.

> *"The cameraman on the film was not very complimentary about George. He thought he probably wasn't up to it, but, hey, that was his opinion. I think he felt that George was a young American who wasn't able to do a film of that size. He was wrong."*
>
> *– Robert Watts*

Through all the turbulence, George Lucas was determined to get the best he could for his movie, which he'd poured so much of his life into. If it was a hit, there would be sequels, he'd promised the crew that. But hardly anyone believed in it, especially the studio financing the picture. And the studio was starting to get a bit jumpy about Lucas's space project, and wanted to rein it in, as 20th Century Fox Executive Peter Beale explains.

> *"Towards the end, we'd gone a couple of weeks over. People were getting a bit tired and tense and my boss Alan Ladd was told by the financers of the company we don't want a 'Cleopatra' here, you're two weeks over. Close the film down in two weeks. And we had four weeks of work to do. Well, first of all, I said to my boss Alan Ladd that it's not possible. We've got four weeks work and his answer was: 'Solve it!' No more. That was it! And I knew him well enough to know that he meant it. So, I went to them and I said, 'We've got a problem, we've got four weeks work to do in two weeks,' and George was obviously very upset."*
>
> *– Peter Beale*

But even though Peter was still young in the industry, he had enough experience to offer a solution.

> "I said, 'Let's pause a moment, let's look at what we've got to do. I think we could do it with two or three units. We can bring another couple of directors on.' And so what happened was Gary Kurtz directed and Robert Watts directed. We had three units working together."
>
> – Peter Beale

With more units shooting, the rolls of film stacked up. The end was almost in sight…well certainly on principal photography. Production Supervisor Robert Watts says all those close to the director believed in him and thought he could get it finished.

> "It wasn't without its ups and downs, but basically it was George Lucas. It was his doing. He was the creative genius. And we were the ones who surrounded him, to help him get this onto the screen."
>
> – Robert Watts

Friendships were also being forged. Friendships that would last a lifetime. Robert Watts remembers inviting Harrison Ford, Mark Hamill, Carrie Fisher and Anthony Daniels to his house for a traditional Sunday roast lunch, even though they were in a middle of a heat wave. After all, it is very British.

> "Harrison, Carrie and Mark, being American, said they hadn't tried Yorkshire puddings before! So on that Sunday, we invited them round for lunch, along with my assistant Pat Carr. I seem to remember there wasn't very much left

on the plates afterwards! And then after we'd had lunch, Mark went into the garden with my children and instigated a water fight! He grabbed the garden hose and they all got soaked. That's Mark, always having fun and the kids loved him. They loved them all."

– Robert Watts

As production moved along at Elstree Studios, the Executive in Charge for Fox, Peter Beale, remembers the very special moment when he actually thought the film might just be a hit!

"I wasn't on the set everyday actually, I used to go a couple of times a week. But I would monitor it, two or three times a day, with Robert on the phone and with Gary. And then there was a moment. I got to the set late one day and noticed there were some children on the set and I thought, 'What's happening here? We don't normally have children on the set,' and I asked whose children they were. And I think they were one of the grip's children and I watched them and they were looking at R2-D2. Absolutely fascinated. They were scared of the Wookiee, they kept a bit back and C-3PO they were looking at, and I thought this is interesting. Then a couple of days later there were more children and the crew started bringing two or three children at a time. And I started to think, 'Well if the children are relating at this level, maybe we have something'."

– Peter Beale

As photography came to an end at Elstree Studios in North London, much of the British element was also coming to an end. Post-production and any pick up shots were to be done in California. More interior cantina scenes were filmed in L.A. That was at the very beginning of 1977, mere months before *Star Wars* would be released in the United States.

Roger Christian explains the approach George took to the movie and the concept he had.

> *"George shot what he needed and put it together. It's a documentary, basically that film, the way that he structured it. It's a documentary about a group of people, that was its kind of breakthrough in cinema."*
>
> *– Roger Christian*

Before filming even began, spending time together meant that they all got an understanding of the young filmmaker's vision. It's certainly what Roger puts their working relationship down to.

> *"It was life-changing for me. Just meeting George, having four months with him, we became friends. We said 'let's go to lunch, let's go to Julie's restaurant', because it was close and it was one of my favourite hangouts. We took George out and you are sitting on sofas in Moroccan surroundings in London; it was the complete opposite of a white tablecloth, classic restaurant. And I think those little things helped George's comfort level with us. It was eclectic stuff."*
>
> *– Roger Christian*

Roger feels that those early moments together, as the director and art department developed mutual respect, would pay off in production.

"George understood immediately that John Barry and I knew what he was talking about. We were like students really and had a common language and knew what we were doing."
— Roger Christian

Well, it was all in the can now. Mostly. George Lucas had put together a very talented group of filmmakers in the U.S. who were working on the models and the special effects. That team, based in California, was the early beginnings of Industrial Light and Magic. And Production Supervisor Robert Watts was in awe of their talents.

"Over in the U.S. they delivered a new form of special effects, called motion control. It was incredible. So it was an Anglo-American co-production. Both sides contributed equally to this wonderful thing that became the 'Star Wars Saga'. But once we'd wrapped in the UK, I kind of felt my role, for the moment at least, was over pretty much on the movie. Of course the post-production was being done in the States, all the editing and all that. And the special effects."
— Robert Watts

There are so many elements that go into making a film: The cast, the crew, the story itself and, of course, the score. There can't be many people on Earth who wouldn't recognise the opening bars of that rousing and emotional score, composed by the legendary John Williams. The American composer would record the soundtrack to *Star Wars* in Britain. And 20th Century Fox Executive Peter Beale was there to witness history in the making.

"For me, probably the most exciting moment of the film was the scoring of the music. It was kind of a wet day and they had the London Symphony Orchestra van outside the studio with its modest little sign on and people carrying in drums and stuff and the musicians turning up and there were two bedraggled girls, sitting on the fence opposite, a little stone fence. I think waiting to see another pop star and being disappointed with all the orchestra stuff coming. And we got into the studio and John Williams was there. John remember was quite young as a conductor/composer. And the famous Lionel Newman of the famous Newman family. And he was there, he was Fox's head of music. The English musicians, early in the morning, always look scruffy and dirty. They've been playing the night before, either in the theatre or in an orchestra and they come in with their tea flasks and their newspapers and they're busy writing down their bets for the day, ignoring everything going on and, after all, as it was only a film score, thinking it wouldn't be too difficult to do. John looked out on them and looked a bit concerned as they were sitting there and he said, 'Lionel, perhaps you'd do the first rehearsal.' So, Lionel went out to do the first rehearsal. And he tapped on the podium, and there was nothing; they carry on chatting and whatever. 'SILENCE!!!' They all looked at him, amazed. He said, 'Put the papers away. Mr. Williams wants a change on bar fifteen.' The lights dimmed and he conducted. It was fantastic."

– Peter Beale

And this was just the beginning of that magical session in the recording studio. Peter was immersed in the sights and sounds of musical history in the making.

> "They did a second rehearsal and made a few more adjustments. And John said, 'I will conduct the actual orchestra.' And John went out. He surprisingly knew all the names of all the leaders, the head of the violins and everything else. Talked to them and told them what he wanted; talked for a few minutes, turned back to Eric the mixer, nodded, lights dimmed, the lights started flashing 5,4,3,2,1 and he started conducting - but not with the baton, but his body. The enthusiasm he got out of the orchestra went to another level. And what he is pulling out of them and subduing them, exciting them, it was just amazing! It was the title music, so it was a long piece of music. And it was just breathtaking. When it finished, the musicians were just transfixed. And John went back into the recording booth where we were watching this extraordinary thing and he did playback. On playback the musicians, who hadn't seen the film, turned around and watched it, it was the title sequence. And at the end, when John went out, they all stood up and applauded with their instruments. Because they recognised that this was something very, very special."
>
> – Peter Beale

Production Supervisor Robert Watts has his own recollection of the time when the maestro, John Williams, conducted the London Symphony Orchestra.

> "It was wonderful. The orchestra was mesmerised by John. And to see them playing the music, along with the movie on the big screen behind them. Well, it was a moment I'll never forget. And then John finished the first session and came into

the sound booth, where we were all watching and listening and he said, 'That's a great band!' Band? Ha ha, it was so funny. Calling the LSO a band. But the orchestra or 'band' certainly performed remarkably for John Williams. The man who made that iconic soundtrack is known and loved the world over!"

— *Robert Watts*

It's a moment Peter Beale holds very dear in his entire film career.

"It was magic. I didn't leave the recording studio in all the time it took to do it and I didn't leave for a second. It was just wonderful. The music provides so much information, emotion, character, drama, tension, anticipation; music is so important. You run a film like 'Star Wars' without it and you're going miss an enormous percentage. Music is very important!"

— *Peter Beale*

CHAPTER SEVEN
Everyone Held Their Breath

(From interviews with
20th Century Fox Executive: Peter Beale
Producer: Gary Kurtz
Set Decorator: Roger Christian
Production Supervisor: Robert Watts
Assistant Art Director: Les Dilley
Costume Designer: John Mollo)

As GEORGE LUCAS toiled in the edit suite and the team at Industrial Light and Magic created breathtaking and groundbreaking scenes, a plan was being hatched to get the movie some hype, before it opened. 20th Century Fox were releasing the picture on May 25th, 1977. And they were hoping to at least make their money back. Fox's man in London, Peter Beale, says some of the excitement around the film was down to a one man marketing campaign.

"A wonderful man called Charlie Lippincott had been working on the underground comics and the underground university film clubs etc. and talking about the film and he

created an awareness that none of us knew about, which was great."

– Peter Beale

During the winter of 1976, while *Star Wars* was in post-production, Charlie Lippincott had been attending science fiction conventions to publicise the movie. Something that Peter Beale thought was very much needed.

"The distribution department for Fox in America were having trouble booking the film, because in those days there were single cinemas. And the other studios were getting the best cinemas and they were having trouble getting the good cinemas for 'Star Wars'. They weren't getting them. And they did some research into the title. And they spent a lot of money researching the words 'Star Wars'. And the research came back saying stars is space and nobody liked space movies. '2001' was intellectual, but nobody wants to go and see a space movie and wars. Vietnam, nobody wants another Vietnam War film. And so the studio said 'we've got to change the title, it's a disaster'. But around the same time, there was a sneak preview in San Francisco, that George Lucas and Gary Kurtz had organised."

– Peter Beale

The movie was ready and Gary thought this would be a good opportunity to gauge the reaction of a real audience.

"We had a preview in May '77 in San Francisco with a general audience, with a mixed bag of people that my office pulled in basically. Everybody from three and four-year-

olds to seventy and eighty-year-olds, just so we would have a cross-section of demographics."

— Gary Kurtz

And Peter Beale remembers that excitement around the preview screening.

"When it was rumoured that there was going to be a sneak preview, people started camping, days before. By the time the preview came, there were lines around the blocks. The publicity department said, 'Oh, it's George paying all his friends to come' but obviously it wasn't because the reaction from it was so enormous. Nobody discussed the title ever again!"

— Peter Beale

Everyone in the test audience for *Star Wars* was given film preview cards, so they could write down what they thought of the movie. But you can't please all of the people all of the time. Not everyone who came to the sneak peek of the movie liked it; in fact, Producer Gary Kurtz recalls a less than favourable review!

"The studio wanted preview cards, we made preview cards. I don't like preview cards myself but they add them up and see what the general reaction is. But you can tell the reaction of an audience just by being in the cinema with them, so I don't think you really need preview cards. But anyway we did it and I still have one of those preview cards on my wall, which was written by a young twenty-something, a film buff, who said: 'This is the worst film I've ever seen since 'Godzilla Vs. The Smog Monster'."

— Gary Kurtz

OK, so not everyone was impressed, but George Lucas's space movie was about to take off! Set Decorator Roger Christian remembers the very first time he laid eyes on the finished movie.

> *"There was a crew screening at the Dominion Theatre in London, at the Tottenham Court Road. And I remember going in there. The music started and when that thing came overhead, I felt the entire cinema almost lift from their seats. Everyone just exploded and you knew then this was going to be a massive hit. Everyone came out buzzing. And we didn't know George could pull off the special effects; before there was World War II footage cut in there. We never knew that this was all going to work."*
>
> *– Roger Christian*

There was definitely a shared feeling of accomplishment among the British art department. They had grafted for George Lucas, under difficult conditions and with very little money. But *Star Wars* had been made and here they were watching the movie, in awe of the collective achievement. For Assistant Art Director Les Dilley it was an unforgettable moment.

> *"I was absolutely amazed, beyond all measure. We knew it was difficult, there was some tricky stuff and unusual stuff. Nobody had seen anything like it. We all wondered about it. But for me it was just magic. Being part of it, it was just incredible for me, it was just a massive education."*
>
> *– Les Dilley*

But if you're looking for one very typical British reaction to seeing their work on the big screen, it's from the Costume Designer, John Mollo, talking as he sips his tea.

"It was quite fun seeing all the bits we'd done, you know and the scenes. We were pleased with what we'd done. Thought it was a good film and good entertainment and all the rest of it, you know. It was a very satisfactory job to do. It was good. Great fun and successful!"

— *John Mollo*

Star Wars premiered in Hollywood in May 1977. Grauman's Chinese Theatre was the cinema that would play host to George Lucas's galaxy. Producer Gary Kurtz remembers fate was on their side when it came to getting that movie theatre.

"The two other big films that were supposed to be out that summer weren't very good. And both fell by the wayside very early. That was the only reason we were able to get into Grauman's Chinese Theatre on Hollywood Boulevard, because that was our target cinema. But it was booked up for 'Sorcerer', which was a remake of 'The Wages of Fear', a French film. But it wasn't ready. So, for May 25th the cinema chain said, 'You can have it for 'Star Wars' for a month, then 'Sorcerer' will be ready.' We said, 'Great, we'll definitely do it.' Fox loved the idea. But they had to have a backup, so after a month they were going to move across the street to another cinema. And we played in there for that month, it was fantastic! We had a big reaction."

— *Gary Kurtz*

Star Wars was much more popular than anyone could have imagined. But Gary says the one thing they hadn't counted on was the way the movie was appealing to a whole range of different people.

> *"In addition to the science fiction audience, which we expected to like the film, it was a crossover film, one that everybody told their friends about and went back to see many times. It's a rousing story, it's fun. It's the kind of film you can see twice in the same day, which many people did. It became a huge hit!"*
>
> *– Gary Kurtz*

The success of *Star Wars* certainly proved it to be the hit George Lucas always hoped it would be. 20th Century Fox had taken some convincing to take a chance on the movie, but now their gamble was about to pay off, as Production Supervisor Robert Watts explains.

> *"20th Century Fox, who were financing the film, didn't believe in it. But when it opened, Fox's price on Wall Street doubled! 'So what can I tell you, 20th Century Fox? I told you so!'"*
>
> *– Robert Watts*

The audiences were coming thick and fast to see *Star Wars*, as it opened in theatres across the U.S. And having the movie play at the iconic Grauman's Chinese Theatre in Hollywood gave it even more kudos. However, as Gary Kurtz recalls, they were only guaranteed a month at the Chinese Theatre. Another movie was due to take its place.

> *"'Sorcerer' came in and we had to move across the street. And the audience was still pretty good for 'Star Wars' and 'Sorcerer' did very little business, it was a difficult film. It was well made, but the story was quite convoluted, the script wasn't very good, so it didn't do very good business. In a month it did less than two or three days of 'Star Wars' busi-*

ness. So they killed it after a month. And asked if we wanted to move back into the Chinese Theatre. We said, 'Absolutely!' So we did and on the day we moved back into the Chinese we decided with Fox that we would have a marketing ceremony. So we have a footprint ceremony on the forecourt of the Chinese cinema where all the handprints and footprints are of the famous stars going back to the 1920s. So we did the robots, we did Darth Vader, and it was a big ceremony. We expected that we might have two or three hundred fans, because the word's going out that we were going to have this ceremony. Well, about five thousand people showed up and filled the street in front of Grauman's Chinese Theatre. It stopped traffic. It was amazing!"

– Gary Kurtz

But Production Supervisor Robert Watts wasn't able to bask in the glory of the success instantly. He was working on another movie in Afghanistan when *Star Wars* hit the theatres.

"I was working in Kabul and we hardly had any communication with the outside world, so I had no idea how successful 'Star Wars' was becoming. My wife and kids had seen it, but I hadn't a clue as to how the whole thing turned out. Then I bought a copy of Time magazine and there, inside, were twelve stunning pictures from the movie and a whole article on the booming success of 'Star Wars'. It was quite a moment."

– Robert Watts

The buzz spread across the Atlantic in less than twelve parsecs, but UK audiences would have to wait an agonising seven months before the film landed. Ironically, the movie that had been made, with so much behind-the-scenes talent from Britain, wasn't to open in London until December 1977. Nevertheless, the talent of those British individuals was now being truly recognised. Robert Watts explains how the success of the production was due to the working relationship between the Brits and their American colleagues, even though there were a few thousand miles between them!

> *"I think a huge amount of it is British and down to British talent. But the guys in America really brought the thing to life with the advent of new technology, that they created to bring us those special effects. And, of course, it was life-changing for us and those little-known American actors at the time, Harrison Ford, Mark Hamill and Carrie Fisher. None of them had done anything before really. Harrison had been in one of George Lucas's movies, 'American Graffiti'. Carrie was nineteen years old. Really young. And I was in my thirties. It was strange, because none of us knew that what we were doing was going to change all our lives, that's all I can say."*
>
> *– Robert Watts*

Peter Beale, the Executive in Charge for 20th Century Fox, never dreamed *Star Wars* would be the runaway success it was.

> *"How COULD you? No film had had that level of success. 'The Omen' had had success. 'The Omen' got to a hundred million dollars and it was made for two point eight; that I thought was fabulous. I thought if we could have got to a hundred I would have been thrilled because it would've been*

profitable. Nobody could have imagined what happened to it, or that it would be a dynasty and carry on and on."

– Peter Beale

For Producer Gary Kurtz, *Star Wars* signified the start of doing things a bit differently.

"I think it gave me a new perspective on the fact that you can try more new things. One of the biggest problems with the film industry in general and still is to this day, is that people aren't very adventurous. They want to make what was popular last year, because they think that will be an easy sell. So you see many sequels of films that shouldn't have sequels. I think that in the case of 'Star Wars' the sequels were actually interesting enough to be viable. But most of the time there are a lot of films that should not be made into sequels but are just because the marketing people say this is an easy sell for us. I'm all for making it easy but I think they need to work harder on this idea of making new things all the time. But looking back, I'm incredibly proud of 'Star Wars'. I think that all of the effort that we put in, trying to get the film off the ground and getting it made paid off really well. It's always a big plus to be involved with a film that turns out to be a big hit. I wouldn't trade it for anything."

– Gary Kurtz

On location in Tunisia, Art Director Les Dilley used his own camera to document the huge task of filming in the desert. (Note the scratch from the negative). (Courtesy of Les Dilley)

Actor Mark Hamill arrives in his Landspeeder to a burning homestead. A crew member can be seen crouching by a very typical 1970s van. (Courtesy of Les Dilley)

In between takes, on the burning homestead scene. (Courtesy of Les Dilley)
(Note the scratch from the negative)

Art Director Les Dilley takes his own shots of the action during filming. This is of Mark Hamill, during a very poignant scene. (Courtesy of Les Dilley)

Another of Les Dilley's personal photographs. Hard to believe that very large piece of set (the dome) actually blew away! (Courtesy of Les Dilley)

Though a dark photograph, it's easy to see it is George Lucas chatting things over with Mark Hamill between takes. (Courtesy of Les Dilley)

Looking down into Luke's home. The 'Gonk' droid and the galaxy of *Star Wars*, juxtaposed with telegraph poles above. (Courtesy of Les Dilley)

A view down a Tunisian street, populated with Stormtroopers and Jawas. On the left of frame, you can see the actor Rusty Goffe, with his 'Gonk' droid legs on! (Courtesy of Les Dilley)

The 'Gonk' droid actor, Rusty Goffe, now has the full outfit on! (Courtesy of Les Dilley)

Luke Skywalker's Landspeeder approaches the spaceport in another of Les Dilley's photographs. (Courtesy of Les Dilley)

In the next shot from Les's collection, you can now see Mark Hamill at the controls, and alongside him legendary British actor, Sir Alec Guinness. (Courtesy of Les Dilley)

"These aren't the droids you're looking for." The heart-stopping moment in *Star Wars* when Obi-Wan Kenobi uses the Force to convince the Stormtroopers they can go about their business. (Courtesy of Les Dilley)

Les Dilley snaps a great shot of Anthony Daniels as C-3PO against the Tunisian sky. (Courtesy of Les Dilley)

In the sweltering heat of the desert, the crew takes a break from constructing the Sand Crawler. To the right of frame, a van from Lee Electrics, driven all the way from London. (Courtesy of Les Dilley)

Everything to build the Sand Crawler was transported to Tunisia and then it's ready to be the backdrop for iconic scenes in the movie. (Courtesy of Les Dilley)

Sir Alec Guinness and Mark Hamill pause during filming, while the crew, behind the camera, look on. George Lucas can be seen looking down, possibly contemplating the next shot. Les Dilley has really captured a moment in movie making history with this picture. (Courtesy of Les Dilley)

R2-D2 makes his way down the slope, before being zapped by the scavenging Jawas. (Courtesy of Les Dilley)

The crew on hand with brooms to make sure Artoo has a smooth ride, avoiding as many obstacles as possible! (Courtesy of Les Dilley)

'Dead' Jawas populate this shot, while Mark Hamill stares at the awesome construction of the Sand Crawler. (Courtesy of Les Dilley)

Sir Alec Guinness and Mark Hamill look on as two members of the film crew make some finishing touches to the Sand Crawler. Crew vans can be seen to the left of the photograph. (Courtesy of Les Dilley)

Mark Hamill stands alone by the Sand Crawler. A long scratch down the picture highlights the standard of personal cameras in the late 1970s. (Courtesy of Les Dilley)

Actor Rusty Goffe waits to get rolling on the next scene as the 'Gonk' droid at the homestead. (Courtesy of Les Dilley)

Actress Shelagh Fraser (Aunt Beru) looks up as Les Dilley snaps another of his behind-the-scenes photographs. (Courtesy of Les Dilley)

From the personal collection of Robert Watts: The production supervisor is chatting with his on screen hero, Sir Alec Guinness, in the blistering heat of Tunisia. On the ground, the back plate of C-3PO. Robert added his own captions to his photograph many years ago! (Courtesy of Robert Watts)

Elstree Studios, late 1970s. (Courtesy of Colin Goudie)

During the filming in London in 1976, Production Supervisor Robert Watts invited some of the actors to Sunday lunch. From left: Production Assistant Pat Carr; Robert Watts; Robert's wife, Julia; and Carrie Fisher. (Courtesy of Robert Watts)

Harrison Ford, Mark Hamill, Anthony Daniels, along with Production Assistant Pat Carr; Production Supervisor Robert Watts and his family, pose for a photograph after Sunday lunch at their house in London in 1976. Carrie Fisher took the picture! (Courtesy of Robert Watts)

A snapshot in time; taken by Robert Watts: A meeting with Concept Artist Ralph MacQuarrie, George Lucas and Art Director Norman Reynolds. (Courtesy of Robert Watts)

December 1977, *Star Wars* is released in London. (Courtesy of Colin Goudie)

Production Designer John Barry and Production Supervisor Robert Watts on the Equator in Kenya. Robert remembers this was a recce for a potential location in The Empire Strikes Back. (Courtesy of Robert Watts)

Art Director Norman Reynolds and Production Supervisor Robert Watts on a recce for filming. (Courtesy of Robert Watts)

During production of *The Empire Strikes Back*, Robert had office signs made for the team. (Courtesy of Robert Watts)

Art Director Les Dilley all wrapped up in his *Empire Strikes Back* crew outfit in Norway. (Courtesy of Les Dilley)

A snatched shot of behind-the-scenes at Elstree Studios, when a young Colin Goudie and friend talked their way onto the set of *Raiders of the Lost Ark*. (Courtesy of Colin Goudie)

Colin Goudie and Gareth Edwards in the edit suite. (Courtesy of Colin Goudie)

Brought together by a mutual love of *Star Wars*, filmmakers Gareth Edwards and Colin Goudie. (Courtesy of Colin Goudie)

Gareth Edwards at the famous homestead of Luke Skywalker in Tunisia. (Courtesy of Gareth Edwards)

As a 30th birthday treat, Director Gareth Edwards travelled to one of the most famous movie locations in the world and sits at Luke Skywalker's dinner table. (Courtesy of Gareth Edwards)

Gareth Edwards at the famous homestead of Luke Skywalker in Tunisia. (Courtesy of Gareth Edwards)

Gareth recreates one of the most iconic shots in *Star Wars*, watching just the one sun setting! (Courtesy of Gareth Edwards)

During filming of *Rogue One* in London, the crew take a break to watch *The Empire Strikes Back* at a secret cinema event. Director Gareth Edwards, Editor Colin Goudie and their friend Luisa Maria Martin couldn't resist dressing up for the occasion! (Courtesy of Colin Goudie)

Gary Kurtz   Peter Beale

Robert Watts (Courtesy of Simon Buck Photography)

John Mollo

Les Dilley

Roger Christian

Nick Maley

Gareth Edwards

Colin Goudie

CHAPTER EIGHT

At the Oscars and Elstree Strikes Back

(From interviews with
Film Editor: Colin Goudie
Assistant Art Director: Les Dilley
Set Decorator: Roger Christian
Creature Maker: Nick Maley)

JUST AFTER CHRISTMAS 1977, *Star Wars* opened in the UK; the Hollywood blockbuster that was actually shot in North London with a host of British talent behind the camera. People queued around the block, outside the cinemas of the capital, with audiences simply desperate to see the movie that had taken America by storm.

But, unlike today where only trailers and snippets of movies are released to promote films, in 1977 it was a different story. Long sections of the film were being shown on the news in Britain, as *Star Wars* fan and Film Editor Colin Goudie remembers.

"You have to remember this is before the days of the internet. This is 1977 and the movie came out in the States in May '77 and it very quickly became the biggest grossing movie of all time, so it was actually a news story. BBC News were running, throughout the summer, all these clips, because British people were involved in the biggest grossing film of all time. So, you'd get interviews with Peter Mayhew on the news and Kenny Baker and they'd keep showing clips of all the exciting action scenes from the movie. It didn't come to the UK until December of 1977, so we'd had to wait seven months and the only places it was showing were two cinemas in London, and I managed to get a ticket for January. It had been out for a couple of weeks, nobody had seen it, none of your friends had seen it because it was just so difficult to get into. So I came down to London, got a ride into town with a friend, went to see it, 70mm Odeon West End, and the first film I'd seen in 70mm and Dolby Stereo and that opening is just mind-blowing! I've never seen anything look this good, or sound this good. I'd never seen spaceships look this real. And then, as the movie unwound, I was a little bit disappointed because every time they got to a big action scene, I'd already seen those clips. A lot, for the previous six months. So it was a double experience of mind-blowing visuals, but, oh, I knew that was going to happen because I'd seen it so many times in those seven months leading up to it. There'd never been any film with that much hype, that could've lived up to it. For me, the 'Star Wars' experience was three years later going to see 'The Empire Strikes Back', where they did the opposite. It was so secretive you didn't know anything!"

– Colin Goudie

Of course, George Lucas had said that if *Star Wars* was a hit there would be sequels. And, true to his word, the director, now famous around the world, was preparing the much-anticipated next chapter, *The Empire Strikes Back*. But this time the way it was financed would be different. Thanks to the explosion of merchandise and the toys, George was making a small fortune. That money meant he could be free of the studio system. 20th Century Fox would distribute the movie, but he was calling the shots. Production Supervisor Robert Watts remembers all too well that Fox had not seen this coming. They had just not banked on the movie being such a runaway success.

> *"It definitely was and they (Fox) messed up in every direction, because not only didn't they believe in it, they had not tied up the sequel rights, nor had they tied up the merchandising rights, so George Lucas owned all of that. So, basically, he owned everything after the first film was out... Bad luck Fox!"*
> *– Robert Watts*

Meanwhile, the behind-the-scenes talent from *Star Wars* was getting the attention of The Academy of Motion Picture Arts and Sciences. The film was nominated for many Oscars in 1978. Among them, John Williams won for Best Original Score; the Sound Designer, Ben Burtt, scooped the Special Achievement Award, and the American special effects team won Best Visual Effects. But the Brits were recognised, too. John Mollo won Best Costume Design and the entire art department walked away with Best Production Design. For Assistant Art Director Les Dilley that was a life-defining moment.

> *"It was exciting, that's one way of putting it; nerve-wracking was another. When you have to walk up to that stage and you are from the UK and in this big arena, it was a big deal.*

> *John Barry was with us, he was the lead, he did the talking. There were four of us. Norman, myself and Roger Christian, the set decorator. That's not bad, but I don't want to sound conceited. When I say things like that, I don't want it to seem conceited. It's just phenomenal for me, that's all."*
>
> *– Les Dilley*

It was a great moment for them all, but one that Set Decorator Roger Christian never thought he'd experience.

> *"We said, 'Well we're not going to win it, we'll just go and enjoy it.' It was science fiction, they thought this is never going to happen. We were sitting in the audience and they'd given it to the special effects boys before; they were all dancing on stage, there were so many of them, thanking dogs and thanking this and all of that. We all sat together and we said, 'John, you speak, this is embarrassing. You just say a few words, if we get it.' It was like a blur. When our names came up, we couldn't believe it! And we went on stage and John basically said thank you very much for this to the Academy and he just looked down at George and said, 'Every single frame of this film belongs to this man there, George Lucas.'"*
>
> *– Roger Christian*

Bob Hope hosted the Academy Awards that year. Roger and the rest of the art department were given their Oscars by actors Greer Garson and Henry Winkler. A surreal experience for Roger.

> *"To most people they didn't give a monkey's **** about me getting an Oscar, it was, 'Wow, what was the Fonz like?' But it was a blur, honestly, and we had to get on the plane*

back because we were in the middle of filming 'Alien'. And at that time, this was 1978, there was not one word in the press about it. Nothing. Worst thing you could do was win an Oscar in Britain. And if you ask any actor who's won, all of these people, they said, 'Oh, I put it in the toilet.' Only you could say you had it in the toilet to hold the door open, otherwise you were a complete ******!"

– Roger Christian

And, according to Roger, not only was there not much press coverage, the celebrations at the London office of 20th Century Fox weren't much either!

"We had a celebration and this will put it into perspective for you. In Peter Beale's office at 20th Century Fox there was John Mollo, me, John Barry, Les Dilley and Norman Reynolds and John Stears and that was it. No celebration whatsoever!"

– Roger Christian

However, that feeling of anti-climax wouldn't last long. Roger Christian and Les Dilley were now working on the look of another science fiction film, *Alien*. Their expertise on bringing the *Star Wars* galaxy to life made them ideal to help with the look of Ridley Scott's science fiction horror film. Meanwhile, work was already underway to get the sequel to *Star Wars* made, *The Empire Strikes Back*. Elstree Studios would once again welcome George Lucas to their stages. And George would welcome back those who had stood by him during the difficult times filming the first *Star Wars* movie. Assistant Art Director Les Dilley was one of those invited back for the next picture.

"He had the same crew for the second one, none of us were aimed out. It was just an amazing time."

— Les Dilley

Production Supervisor Robert Watts had impressed George Lucas; they'd become friends. Robert was also hired for the sequel.

"It's very much like having an extended family because many of the people are the same. And it is always like that, because we work closely together. It's creative work and I suppose you could say we love each other."

— Robert Watts

But Robert remembers that love between him and Harrison Ford was almost put to the test, over a scene in Norway.

"We had to find a location for the ice planet of Hoth, somewhere covered in snow, but without trees. We found this incredible place in Norway called Finse. And we were filming in a blizzard. Well, we were going to shoot Han Solo's scenes in a blizzard at Elstree, but here we were, all the crew in Norway in a blizzard, for real. So, I called London and said, 'Get Harrison on the next flight to Oslo.' I then sent the location manager down to Oslo on a snow plough, because all the trains couldn't run due to the storm. I sent him down and I said, 'Bring Harrison up here, here's a bottle of whiskey for him, too.' So off he went. All the crew went to bed but I waited up and eventually Harrison arrived at one in the morning, I think. He'd had some of the whiskey! And he stormed into the hotel and saw me and said, 'Call my agent!' and I was a bit worried, but then he started laughing! He was teasing me.

And I had to get him to film the next morning and, bless him, I will always be grateful to him, he was brilliant!"

– Robert Watts

Filming in Norway certainly came with its challenges but once back at Elstree Studios there would, of course, be more, as the latest *Star Wars* movie was breaking even more boundaries. One of the biggest sets at Elstree would be the swamp-like world of Dagobah, home to the exiled Jedi Master, Yoda, a character that would win the hearts of *Star Wars* fans. Les Dilley helped build the ambitious set, but his desire to get everything just right, left him… a little damp!

"I was out on the set and I was responsible for R2-D2, amongst other things. We were on the bog planet. R2-D2 is there on the bank and the aircraft behind them in the water and they haven't got it out yet. They are struggling to get it out. I've got R2-D2, I am responsible for him and we are on this little island and the camera crew is behind me, the actors are in front of me and R2-D2. The crew says, 'OK Les put his head on.' So, I put the head on and click it on and make sure his lights are working. And, of course, being the sort of man I am, I take a step back to take a look to see how everything looks. I stepped back and I fell right in the water of the bog planet in front of the whole crew. And this is the studio, the studio where I was an apprentice from fifteen years old. Well, my name went round that studio: 'Les Dilley has fallen in the bog tank!' You never saw somebody falling into water get out so quick!"

– Les Dilley

Dagobah would be the location where Luke Skywalker meets his mentor and teacher of the Force, Yoda. But the green puppet had to be believable, it had to be convincing. The audience had to think this puppet was the most powerful Jedi in the galaxy. Nick Maley, having proved himself to creature maker Stu Freeborn on *Star Wars*, was in the workshop once more for *Empire*.

> *"We were going through a difficult period at that time. We'd gone through several months of deciding what Yoda was going to look like. And we'd used half our production time on just that. Then we had several weeks where we were making the moulds and foaming the pieces to have something to work with. And Stu, all that time, had been working on the prototype mechanism. You've got to remember Yoda was the world's first animatronic superstar. No one had built a puppet that sophisticated before. Stu was trying to make an extraordinary eye mechanism, which would allow Frank Oz's hand to move through. And there were various problems that showed themselves up in the first week of filming. It had certain 'hiccups.' Stu eventually sorted all of those out. But there were hold-ups in the shooting and, as a result, Stu was standing by all day to fix it when it broke down. And then working all night, to try and solve the problems. It came to a culmination one morning when Robert Watts was banging on the door to try to get Yoda on the set, and Yoda wasn't put back together."*
> – Nick Maley

Every hour counted, every hour cost and Production Supervisor Robert Watts had a film crew hanging around, waiting to shoot scenes with Yoda and Mark Hamill.

> "Well, Stuart Freeborn, who was our makeup guy, he was having terrible trouble getting Yoda into working condition. He'd overdone it to the extent that the day we were going to shoot on Yoda, I go up there and it's all in pieces. And I had Nick Maley on the show as well who is good at that kind of stuff."
>
> – Robert Watts

Nick Maley knew this was his chance to prove himself to his colleagues.

> "It was agreed that I should take some of the parts that we had made, that were lying around, and try to put together a backup Yoda. I told him (Robert Watts) to give me three days. And I told him I would make something that at least he could shoot the back of the head, that would have working ears. But ultimately I knew this was my moment. This was that opportunity where I was going to have to show what I could do. And so what I wanted to do was make something that did everything. I built what I would call a pretty rough mechanism. But it was built in three days. I took part of an eye mechanism and finished that. We went down the road to the bicycle shop and bought bike brake cables. We had to get whatever we could lay our hands on and he had eight bike brake cables hanging through his body. And we stayed there for sixty hours, working day and night. Bob Keen, who was one of the trainees, he worked with me and I slept on the floor, while he did some soldering. Then he slept on the floor while I was doing some finishing. Ultimately it was that moment that was either going to make me or break me."
>
> – Nick Maley

To this day Robert Watts is still impressed with how Nick took the initiative and got the puppet ready and working so it could be filmed and complete the scenes for *The Empire Strikes Back*.

> *"Nick took it over and put it together and got it to work. And this is nothing against Stuart, he was one of the most fantastic people and did the most fantastic, extraordinary work, but Nick in that moment came and you know that happens all the time. We all help each other. Nick got Yoda working!"*
>
> *– Robert Watts*

And we all know the scene where their work came to fruition. The one where Yoda has just met Luke for the very first time. Watching the raw footage was a defining moment for Nick Maley.

> *"It was Yoda with his head in the box, throwing all this stuff over his shoulder. That was an extraordinary moment. It wasn't that I saw him on set because when we got him and took him down to Frank (Oz) we went to the workshop, we were too tired to drive. So we went to the workshop and slept in the storeroom. Just slept on the floor. And when we woke up, we'd slept for something like twenty-something hours and they had the rushes. Rushes are silent pieces of film from the previous day. We went into the viewing theatre and there were only five of us there. There was George Lucas sitting forward with the cinematographer. I knew at that moment that we'd done something that no one would ever forget. It's very hard for me to tell that story without getting emotional because it was THE turning point in my career. It was the culmination of 13 years' work."*
>
> *– Nick Maley*

Nick pays tribute to Stu Freeborn and says it was thanks to his guidance that the team was able to bring the creatures to life.

"Stuart was the mastermind behind all the creatures and Stuart was the guy who was really Yoda's dad. Legend has it that Yoda is 900 years old, but he was actually born in 1978 in Elstree, on the outskirts of London. The ideas that came from America were great, but actually we didn't end up following any of those illustrations; they were influenced by what came up, but what Stu sculpted, which I thought was brilliant, was really quite different from what was originally designed."

– Nick Maley

Stuart Freeborn, sometimes known as the 'grandfather of modern make-up design', was instrumental in leading the creature workshops on the *Star Wars* movies. He died in 2013. Nick attributes much of the success of his own career to Stu Freeborn.

"Stu was the old man of creature effects in England. I spent two years basically stalking him, trying to get him to let me carry his bag. I was just a new guy who had a union ticket, but wasn't getting any work. If I hadn't worked with him, then my whole career would not have happened. He was quite a hard taskmaster but he had done so much stuff going all the way back to 'Oliver Twist', 'Doctor Strangelove' and '2001: A Space Odyssey'. I knew he was going to get all the best jobs. I would've worked for him for nothing. And the things that I learned there. As a really effective creature effects person you have to be imaginative, you have to be able to develop things, but you need to be fed the information to know which direction to go in and how to develop. A lot

of the things I did later on were entirely based on what I learned from Stu."

— *Nick Maley*

Star Wars had certainly boosted a lot of careers. It was the break many on the crew had been waiting for.

Production Supervisor Robert Watts had seriously impressed his boss, George Lucas. And he was about to be trusted with another box office smash!

"We'd just finished shooting 'The Empire Strikes Back' and I was over in America, ILM, the LucasFilm place in San Rafael. We were just doing a few pick-ups and George came on the stage one morning and he said, 'Have a look at this, Robert.' And he handed me a script that was called 'Raiders of the Lost Ark'. He said, 'Let me know what you think.' So, I went back that night and I read it. I came in the next day and I said, 'My God George, this is a busy movie!' 'Oh,' he said, 'well this is the next film I want to do, Steven Spielberg's going to direct it.' Well I'd never met Steven Spielberg at this point. George said, 'You should go down to L.A. and meet him, because I want you on it, but you've got to meet Steven.' So, I went down to L.A. and I met Steven Spielberg."

— *Robert Watts*

At this point, Robert's career was really taking off. Having started out in the industry as a runner, he was now on a trajectory that would take him to new heights in the movies.

"Well I kept getting promoted up the ranks and I finally got full producer credit on 'Indiana Jones and the Temple of

Doom'. The second of the 'Indiana Jones' films and that was an extraordinary thing!"

– Robert Watts

For Assistant Art Director Les Dilley, who'd been an apprentice on the sets when he was younger, his career was also now in the fast lane. He'd join Norman Reynolds and Robert Watts on *Raiders of the Lost Ark*. But before that, he'd been with old *Star Wars* pal, Roger Christian, on *Alien*.

"Working with Ridley Scott was astonishing. That director, that man's just a brilliant technician, a clever artist, knows the business inside and out. He knows how to do it all."

– Les Dilley

On *Raiders* Les would discover that being an art director would mean getting his hands dirty, again! He had to help push that famous boulder that chases Harrison Ford down a tunnel in the opening scene.

"Well, we got it all rigged up, because it starts very high up on a track coming down and it stops; well, it doesn't actually stop, it's going in the scene but it actually stops and it's rolling down on its own, on the floor. And it's still got to chase Harrison Ford and of course the ball is pretty big. And three of us had to be behind it, pushing it, to chase him. We were all out of energy by the time we finished!"

– Les Dilley

By this time, the British movie industry was booming once more. *Star Wars*, *The Empire Strikes Back*, *Return of the Jedi* were all shot at Elstree. And thanks to the relationship Robert Watts had with the studio, *Raiders of the Lost Ark*, *The Temple of Doom* and *The Last Crusade* were filmed there, too.

And sneaking onto one of these movie's sets would help fuel a young filmmaker's passion. A passion for film, which would eventually lead to him working on a *Star Wars* movie himself!

CHAPTER NINE

The Force is Strong with the Next Generation

(From interviews with
Film Editor: Colin Goudie
Director: Gareth Edwards)

STAR WARS HAD definitely changed cinema forever. It had everything, all of the ingredients needed to make the perfect movie. Heroes, villains, groundbreaking special effects, a rousing soundtrack and sequels to boot! It proved, beyond a shadow of a doubt, that it was far more than just a science fiction film. It transcended genres and people who'd never even liked sci-fi loved *Star Wars*! It was shaping a generation and for a few of those mesmerised by what they saw on the silver screen, it would be the reason why they set their hearts on becoming part of the industry.

Film Editor Colin Goudie remembers how *Star Wars* really opened his eyes to film.

"'Star Wars' got me really into sci-fi, even more than I had been. I just wanted to make films like 'Star Wars' myself. I'd go out into my garage, build little Airfix models and then blow them up!! Literally, with fireworks and things. And try and make little sci-fi films. I was 16 when I saw 'Star Wars' for the first time and I'd just left school and I'd gone to art college and I got fascinated with all the artwork of all the designers from those movies and I'd buy the art of 'Star Wars', I'd buy all the blueprints from 'Star Wars', Ralph McQuarrie paintings. There was very limited merchandising available in those days, so every little tiny piece on that side I would gravitate towards and spend my wages on buying those things. And by the time 'Empire' came out, I was at Bournemouth Film School and then it was like everyone was making sort of quite gritty, realistic films about relationships and I wanted to make films where you blew up space stations! It definitely lit a spark in my heart that I've sort of followed ever since really."

– Colin Goudie

While Colin was blowing up his Airfix models and trying to replicate the incredible special effects of Industrial Light and Magic, somewhere else in Britain, Nuneaton to be precise, a young boy was getting hooked on that galaxy, far, far away.... A young boy, who grew up to be Film Director Gareth Edwards.

"I don't actually remember the first time I saw it. The first memory I have was that my parents drove me to a car park next to the Co-Op, in my hometown Nuneaton. And they said, 'We've got a surprise, you should come with us.' I didn't

want to. I didn't want to hang out with my parents on a Saturday. And they were like, 'No, you've got to come,' so we go in the car and we park and I wait and they go into whatever store it was. I don't even know which one it was. And they come out about half an hour later and they have a Betamax player. And I think we bought an ex-rental one, this secondhand thing. And we go back home and as we're driving home, my dad reminds me, or tells me that our next-door neighbour has a copy of 'Star Wars'. And I was like, 'OK, oh my God,' and so I go round to the neighbour and I do my best sheepish kind of polite boy impression and say, 'Excuse me, would it be possible to borrow 'Star Wars'? I promise I will bring it back after we've watched it.'"

– Gareth Edwards

An excited young Gareth Edwards then raced back home, clutching the Betamax cassette of *Star Wars*. What he was about to experience, he would remember forever.

"I put it in. And I hit play, and it was the opening scene. It got to Threepio and I think it got as far as the desert, with the crashed pod and Threepio and Artoo, and my mum calls me for my dinner, and I stop it. I run to the table, eat as fast as I can, and I just think, 'I know what I'm going to do for the rest of my life. I'm going to watch that film over and over and over until I die. That would be the perfect life for me right now, no one can take this away. I've got this tape, no one can steal it and I can watch 'Star Wars' anytime I want.' And I never ever took it back! It just hit a nerve and it felt really weird to be two years old, or whatever you were, and

feel like and know deep down like, 'I think I've just watched the best story that I can ever be told, this is perfect. This just feels totally right and I don't really know for the rest of my life if I'm going to find a better one.'"

– Gareth Edwards

While Gareth was glued to his TV watching his, or rather his neighbour's copy of *Star Wars* virtually on a loop, Colin Goudie was doing his utmost to get on the set of the sequel to *Empire: The Return of the Jedi.*

"So I saw there was a film being shot at Elstree Film Studios, which was where they'd filmed 'Star Wars' and 'The Empire Strikes Back', being made by LucasFilm, starring Harrison Ford. I thought, 'This has got to be the next 'Star Wars' film. It has to be!' There's not going to be a three-year wait. I have to get on the set of that movie. I used to write film reviews for my local college magazine, so I could get into the cinema for free, because I was quite poor! So I phoned up Elstree Studios and I said I was a journalist, British journalist, writing an article on the British film industry and could I come and visit Elstree studios and they said, 'Yes.' My best friend Mike who was also at college and he was an animator and he stood next to me and went, 'And me!' and I asked, 'Can I bring a photographer?' And they said, 'Yes, of course!' So I borrowed a suit, borrowed a briefcase, shaved off my studenty beard. I borrowed a brolly; I thought if I look like John Steed, I might look like I was a professional journalist. We took the train down to Elstree Studios, got in, were met by the Head of Elstree Studios, who took us on a tour. As we

> *walked in, he said, 'OK, so we're filming some movies here at the moment, we're filming 'The Shining' which is directed by Stanley Kubrick, but that's a closed set, so you can't go on that. And we're filming the John Reed, Louise Bryant story with Warren Beatty (which came out as the film 'Reds'), that's a closed set, you can't go on that.' And I thought I know how this is going to go and he said, 'But we're filming a George Lucas-produced film, directed by Steven Spielberg, called 'Raiders of the Lost Ark', would you like to visit that set?' And I didn't hesitate, 'Yes! That would be fantastic.'"*
>
> – Colin Goudie

Colin and his chum had blagged their way in. They were being taken on a guided tour of Elstree and the one and only Steven Spielberg was directing this film they were being told about. A George Lucas Production, Harrison Ford, Spielberg: it had to be the third installment of *Star Wars*, right?

> "*So he took us onto the sets of 'Raiders', that they'd previously filmed on, that they hadn't yet demolished, because they were waiting for rushes clearance and he says, 'So the archaeologist comes here and he takes this idol off this thing here which causes this entire set to collapse, and this was a practical set that we built.' And he's described this entire thing and Mike and I are thinking, 'This doesn't sound like 'Star Wars' at all. Maybe this is not the sequel to 'The Empire Strikes Back'.' Then our guide says, 'Would you like to come onto the 'Well of Souls' set?' We went onto the set and there were all these snakes and there was the sequence as they were knocking over the jackal into the wall and Steven Spielberg*

was up in the ceiling on his camera rig filming. It was, at that point, the best day of my life!"

— Colin Goudie

OK, so it wasn't the *Star Wars* secret, but, for Colin, somebody who was at film school, to actually be on a LucasFilm set, it was just incredible. It helped to inspire Colin further and, after film school, he joined the British Broadcasting Corporation, a move that would eventually lead him to a friendship and partnership with Gareth Edwards.

"I left film school, I graduated from Bournemouth, managed to get a job at the BBC as a trainee assistant film editor, back in the days when there were traineeships. I worked at the BBC for ten years and managed to make my way up from trainee to assistant and then to dubbing editor, to film editor. We were literally physically cutting on film. Exactly the same as 'Raiders' would have been cut. So that's what we did, we edited on 35mm and Super 16 and also learned video tape editing, which was this new thing that was coming in. And then I went freelance after ten years at the BBC. And I worked on documentaries and drama. I used to work mainly on drama series and documentaries, they were my two specialities. And occasionally one-off single, made-for-TV films."

— Colin Goudie

Colin's career course was setting him on a path that would mean he was racking up oodles of experience, experience that would stand him in good stead for a future in feature films. A path that Gareth Edwards was desperate to get on, too.

The Force is Strong with the Next Generation

"I watched 'Star Wars' and I thought, 'OK, my plan A in life is to join the Rebel Alliance and help blow up the Death Star.' Then eventually people tell you, 'It's not real, it doesn't really exist, it's this thing called a film' and so you think, 'OK, Plan B, is I will become a filmmaker.'"

– Gareth Edwards

And for Gareth, discovering that *Star Wars* was shot in Britain, gave him that extra boost. Though when he first learnt that it had been made in the UK, it came as a bit of a surprise, to say the least.

"I think as a kid you picture it in this galaxy far, far away. And it's a real shock to learn one day it was actually somewhere just off the M25. And kind of depressing. You go, 'That can't be right. Someone's made a mistake. Maybe it's the Galaxy M25.' I think there is one called that. But then the upside of that is, 'OK, that means I could do this, this is in my country, if I get a job in London.' And I do remember my first job in television. I had to work on this TV show that was filmed at Bushey in North London and you have to go really early, like at 5 AM. And I would get in a cab from the train station. And I'm holding a tripod and a camera. And for whatever reason, the cabbie has done these trips all day long. All morning long, because of auditions and things and goes, 'Alright mate, you going to the 'Star Wars' set?' And I suddenly realised, 'Oh yeah, they're filming Episode One in London. And he thinks I'm part of the crew.' I wanted to go, 'Yes, yes I'm filming 'Star Wars', take me there now. And don't worry about security, just keep going'. And it was really depressing to go: 'No, I'm doing a TV show soap opera-type

thing, it's at the different place.' And so, I didn't get to go but it was very tangible that 'Star Wars' is just over there. You can do it."

– Gareth Edwards

Knowing that the original *Star Wars* trilogy was shot in London, and with *The Phantom Menace* and the other prequels being filmed here, Gareth was now bristling with enthusiasm. He was determined he would get into making movies, one way or another.

"I was in a section of the BBC called 'Specialist Factual' which is a fancy word for documentaries. And then there was the drama department, and the two worlds didn't really interact when I was there, and what was really interesting about Specialist Factual is that through science documentaries they were developing a relationship with computer graphics, because they had to show how molecules worked, or DNA, or how planets orbited the sun. So they were very used to dealing with visual effects companies and getting them to animate things for their shows. And then, as computers get better and better and more and more real, the things that these companies can offer get more advanced. They could create a city, they can do all these Hollywood production values, and so the factual department started doing these things called drama-docs, which were like kind of a poor man's drama in a way, but the scope of them would look bigger than what the drama department was doing. And at the time I was doing computer graphics and I was kind of working from home. I went to study film, I basically did a film degree at university and thought, 'OK, when I graduate I'll send my short film to

Hollywood and then they'll phone up and offer me a feature film.' That's the way it worked for Spielberg. And so obviously that's how it's going to work for everyone else, right? And then I didn't get that call. Nothing happened!"

– Gareth Edwards

But getting his head around the emerging technology of computer graphics and animation would be the leg up Gareth needed to getting noticed.

"This was like '93 to '96 so 'Jurassic Park' had just come out. So, I bought a computer and stacked shelves in Marks & Spencer at night and in the day I was trying to learn the software. Every time I went for an interview, I would show my show reel and at the end tag on these effects shots, which were like a dinosaur in the street or a robot running down my parents' driveway, and they'd get to the end and go, 'What is all this stuff?' And you'd say, 'Oh, it's just something I did on my home computer.' And this is 1997 and they'd go, 'Well you can't do that on a home computer' and you'd say, 'Yes, you can.' And they'd say, 'Hang on, well we're paying millions to do this down the road,' and you'd think, 'Well, that's your problem, you can do it!' Moore's law is this thing to do with computers, which is every eighteen months to two years computers get twice as fast, we're all familiar with it. Computers have just been getting better and better and so what it used to cost to make, you know, special effects, like dinosaurs in 'Jurassic Park', your iPhone is probably more powerful than the computers they made 'Jurassic Park' with. So you can kind of do this stuff from home. So I started try-

ing to do that and I didn't get jobs directing, I got jobs doing computer graphics for these BBC shows. Doing all like, I used to call it 'disaster porn'."

– Gareth Edwards

Gareth Edwards, the man who would become only the second British director of a *Star Wars* movie, had his foot in the door.

"I did loads of them. I did the VFX on a lot of 'Horizons' and things and I really enjoyed it. It might have been the age I was, but it was one of the best times of my life. I'd work from home, where you are your own boss. And then once a week it would be like, you've got to go to this country and supervise this shoot we're doing and I ended up going all over the place. I went to Panama, Bulgaria, Poland, and New York and California."

– Gareth Edwards

Now you'd be forgiven for thinking Gareth, being the effects guy, would get the time to be able to do his job on location. But that's not the way he remembers it.

"As the VFX supervisor, or whatever you are, you're kind of nobody on the film set. You're sort of stood there, trying to get little things that are going to make your life easier in post-production, but on set, things are so crazy. It definitely got you used to hanging around with a crew. As the VFX guy, you would be stood around all day and you'd get your little window of like, 'OK, you've got ten minutes, what do you need?' And they'd let you shoot stuff. And over to the side I always had this portable green screen and I would get the

> *background artists and extras to do these kind of loop-able walk cycles and things, so I could populate the background with even more. And you'd always be trying to convince the producer, like 'If you just give me five people I can give you like a thousand people back, like in the backgrounds,' but they would never have the time or the resources to give you the five people. There's often a feeling in production which is screw the visual effects, we've just got to get this film shot and done, and then all that problem of doing all the computer graphics gets pushed downstream and then everyone disappears and goes away and does another film and then the filmmakers are stuck, trying to fix this thing in post."*
>
> *– Gareth Edwards*

However, slaving away over his hot computer at home, fixing things in post, was the very thing that would lead to a friendship for life and a filmmaking partnership. And the moment Gareth walked into Colin Goudie's edit suite at the BBC, they clicked.

> *"I met Colin doing a BBC series called 'Space Race'. I came in and delivered some computer graphics to him, some visual effects shots of these Russian spacecraft and I suddenly walked in and he had all these things around his edit suite that were sci-fi and 'Star Wars' related. And I was like: 'This is the kind of thing I would do if I was an editor,' and then I gave him all the stuff and it would take ten minutes to give the shots and go, 'Any notes, anything you want me to change?' then you'd leave. But I must've stayed there like the first time for two hours and we were just chatting about films and our favourite movies and science fiction, I guess.*

And I left and I thought, 'I really like that guy' and then every time I came to drop VFX off, we'd chat for hours and get no work done."

– Gareth Edwards

Colin recalls when he met Gareth at the BBC and how their shared love of *Star Wars* was about to forge a friendship that would eventually take them around the world, shooting the kind of movie they both adored.

"'Space Race' was a BBC four-part drama series about the Americans and the Russians race to the moon. And the VFX supervisor was a guy called Gareth Edwards, who was twenty-nine years old, and we got on really well because my edit suite was always full of 'Star Wars' toys."

– Colin Goudie

But Gareth was about to out-*Star Wars* Colin Goudie, if that was indeed possible, as he was about to make a serious fan pilgrimage to the locations that were used as the desert planet, Tatooine.

"Gareth said, 'Oh, it's my 30th birthday and I'm going to go to Tunisia to visit all the 'Star Wars' locations, so I won't be around to do your VFX for the next couple of weeks.' I thought, 'This sounds like the greatest trip ever!'"

– Colin Goudie

A slightly envious Colin stayed behind in London, while his newfound *Star Wars* mate journeyed to Tunisia. It was certainly one off the bucket list for Gareth.

The Force is Strong with the Next Generation

"I stayed the night in Luke Skywalker's house in Tunisia and I watched the sun set by the igloo on the salt flats and all that."

— *Gareth Edwards*

Just one sun, of course! And on returning to London, he had a very special gift for Colin. One only a true fan would understand.

"I remember Gareth came back after his two weeks in Tunisia for his 30th and he had little 35mm film canisters, the clear ones, and in them were dirt. Sand and little bits of rock and he said, 'This is the sand from outside Ben Kenobi's house. And this is the sand and the rock from the canyon where R2-D2 gets hit by the Jawas and falls over.' And he'd literally matched up his photographs and gone to the exact place where Artoo had collapsed. And I went, 'This is so cool.' And Gareth went, 'I knew you'd get this. Nobody else gets it; my girlfriend didn't get it, nobody else gets it.' And he gave them to me, they're on my mantelpiece at home with my 'Star Wars' collection."

— *Colin Goudie*

Gareth Edwards and Colin Goudie are certainly kindred spirits when it comes to *Star Wars;* uber geeks, loving the movies together. Colin explains that being that deeply into *Star Wars* was their common bond, something which would run through all that they would do together in the future.

"Gareth's so much younger than I am that for him he'd grown up with them as a child, they were his childhood movies. And I think to find somebody that was that bit older

who was just as big a geek as he was, I think he felt a little bit more adult, by meeting somebody who was an adult who was also a huge 'Star Wars' fan. After 'Space Race' Gareth and I always stayed in touch, we'd go to the cinema together, whenever there was a big sci-fi movie coming out, we would be texting: 'Do you want to go and see 'Watchmen'? Do you want to go and see 'War of the Worlds'?' We both love Spielberg. And then Gareth made a film for the BBC called 'Attila the Hun'. The BBC producers I'd worked with previously, they phoned me up and they said, 'Gareth Edwards is directing a one-off historical epic for us and we'd like to know if you'd be interested in being the editor?' And I said absolutely, I totally want to do this. And they then started to continue to give me the double-glazing salesman pitch as to why I should do this film. I said, 'No, you had me at Gareth Edwards.' I went off to Bulgaria and we made this film called 'Attila the Hun' for the BBC. Gareth did all the visual effects himself; it had more visual effects per hour than 'Lord of the Rings' and it was made for about a million pounds. So not a small budget, but for what we were making and what was on screen it was phenomenal."

— Colin Goudie

Editing alongside the director can be a fractious relationship, especially over decisions that will affect the outcome of the film. But, as Colin explains, neither of them had any concerns about how they would get along in their new working relationship.

"That was the first time I'd been working with him in the relationship where Gareth was the director and I was his

editor. Previously he'd been my VFX guy doing VFX for me. So could we survive that change in the relationship? Which we totally could. Gareth is such fun in an edit suite, he really is. I mean, you work incredibly long hours, but the days do go by very quickly because he's a really great guy to work with. He's very funny, makes a joke of everything. And my wife was an editor as well; sometimes she would come into the edit suite while we were working together and she would say, 'You two get a room, because you're the married couple. It's not us, you're the married couple'."

– Colin Goudie

But this marriage of minds, brought together through mutual work and a passion for *Star Wars*, was about to be put to the test. The next project for the dynamic duo was their first feature together but with very little money! Sound familiar? Yet it only came about after Gareth got fired. In fact, it turned out to be the kick start he needed.

CHAPTER TEN
Monsters and Going Rogue

(From interviews with
Film Editor: Colin Goudie
Director: Gareth Edwards)

As the old saying goes, as one blast door closes, another one opens... Well, you hope it does. Gareth Edwards and Colin Goudie were now firm friends through their love of sci-fi, but mainly *Star Wars*. They wanted to make their own science fiction movie. Gareth had won a competition with a short called 'Factory Farmed', which he'd made in his spare time.

> *"I entered this 48-hour film competition, where you have to make a film in two days. And I did all the effects on it at home."*
> *– Gareth Edwards*

It was a very quick turnaround. The film is about a bleak future where humans are born on clone farms, a thread that runs throughout his favourite movie franchise, of course. 'Factory Farmed' was also released on May the Fourth (2008), another coincidence?

Perhaps. But Gareth's continued path to feature films would first mean he was going to lose his job.

> *"I got fired from a Discovery Channel show. I got to do even bigger TV shows, which I think was about a two-and-a-half-million-pound budget TV special, about a meteor destroying the Earth and I was on it just for a few weeks and then someone came to visit me from high up at Discovery and basically he said, 'Gareth I'm sorry, we want someone with more experience.' I was like, 'Oh, OK, there's nothing I can do about that.' And they said, 'Really sorry, we're going to get another director.'"*
>
> *– Gareth Edwards*

Having risen up in the TV world as a director, things had just come crashing down. But as a very dejected Gareth Edwards was leaving Discovery, fate intervened.

> *"As I left, one of the executives, who was really nice, felt really bad and said, 'You should get an agent and I know this lady and you should go talk to her.' So, I went and met this woman called Amanda and we got on really well and I explained my situation and she says, 'Well, there's this company in London that specialises in low budget filmmaking, feature films. You should go chat with them.' And so I go and visit them, eventually I show them my show reel of visual effects, which were all done from my bedroom. And I was like, 'It cost like a hundred quid, this is like the computer graphics you can do from home. Someone's going to make a film from their bedroom that is going to look like it cost millions, when really it cost hundreds. We should be the first ones to*

do it,' and they bought into this and were really excited. And they said, 'Great when do you want to start filming?'"

– Gareth Edwards

The company, Vertigo, was really impressed with Gareth, but the young filmmaker couldn't quite believe what was happening.

"I thought, 'OK, I'm going to be one of those stories, this is not real.' And so James, who was one of the producers, said, 'I promise you it's real, write down a date you want to start filming and you'll be filming on that date.' So I did some quick math: I run out of money in three months and so I wrote down three months away and he goes, 'OK, alright.' I didn't have a screenplay, I didn't have anything; we didn't even know what the film was about. And so I had three months to figure out the entire movie, or as much as I could."

– Gareth Edwards

Helping to figure out the movie with Gareth would be his friend, Colin Goudie.

"After 'Attila', Gareth then was offered, by Vertigo Films, to make a low budget movie, science fiction film, called 'Monsters'. He asked me if I would come with him to make this film and instead of having a crew of about a hundred, which we had on 'Attila', and he hadn't enjoyed that experience at all because he wanted to put the camera here, all the Winnebagos had to move, all the catering trucks had to move, and the time would go by and the light would go and he'd be like, 'Why are we not filming?' He was very frustrated by that process, so he said, 'What I want to do is

just take you and me, a laptop and a camera, two actors, producer, translator and we're going to travel around Mexico and Central America and make a science fiction film.'"

– Colin Goudie

The small team, if you could even call them that, was starting to form a plan of how they were going to make *Monsters*. It would mean Gareth going about things in his own way, especially as they only had three months to pull everything together.

"By the time we got to Mexico we had the whole structure, but I didn't write a screenplay. I wrote like a paragraph for each scene and the reason was I didn't want to get too specific, that's when it gets expensive. So if you say, 'Oh, they sat on a black leather chair, in a particular office, overlooking Los Angeles or whatever,' someone will have to go to the trouble of 'Oh, we can't find a leather chair, so we'll have to buy one and to get permission in L.A.' and all those details are not really important. It's what the scene's about that's important. And so I wrote what the scene was about and felt like where it is and how it works, we'll just figure out on the spot. It could be in a bar, it could be on a train, it could be in a harbour. Whatever. But I won't get that anal about the actual geography of it. So we wrote it like that and we drove round Mexico and we ended up in Belize and Guatemala, Costa Rica and Texas. And we kind of did this journey that the characters in the film do. Whenever we got somewhere we would ask the locals, 'Is there anything really strange, that's visually interesting?' After a while, after they understood what you meant, they'd be like, 'Oh, there was a flood.

If you just go down this road and take a left, you'll see there's this whole place flooded, or if you just keep going the road got destroyed - or there's a forest fire or there's a big festival tomorrow night where there's these candles.' They just say stuff and you'd go, 'OK, cool,' then you'd look through the document that I'd written and go, 'OK, maybe this is like the protest,' you know what I mean? And in my head, as you're filming, I'm thinking. And we ended up at this thing called The Day of the Dead Festival and it's all these candles and it's a really beautiful thing the locals do, where they go and visit the graves of their family. But I'm filming it, picturing replacing signs with like these protest ideas. And like people who've been killed in our movie. In the car park of Vertigo, as like a pick up shoot later, I filmed these framed photos of people who worked in the office and some candles in the foreground. And then intercut that with the real footage."

– Gareth Edwards

And there was a serious amount of footage, too. So quite handy that the editor, Colin Goudie, was on location to go through it.

"Gareth was the writer of 'Monsters', he was the director, he was the cinematographer, production designer and he did the visual effects. The movie was improvised by the two actors. So they would take Gareth's story and they would literally ad-lib every single take and then they gave me one hundred-plus hours of footage!"

– Colin Goudie

In post-production, using visual effects, Gareth would replace anything that was out of place and put in something that was relevant to the story line.

> *"Really, we were just reverse engineering whatever we got into the film. And it felt like a really great way to approach filmmaking."*
>
> *– Gareth Edwards*

Once *Monsters* was finished, it was time for Gareth's very first feature to be shown to the world… Well, a few hundred people at least. Someone would be interested, right?

> *"We finished the movie, we sent it to Sundance and Berlin Film Festivals. And it got rejected from all of them. And we ended up at a festival called South by Southwest, in Texas. We ended up at a midnight screening, our world premiere was a midnight screening, in a cinema that fits I think about two hundred people. In the middle of the screening the projector broke. It was really depressing, it felt like it was broken for about ten minutes, but Colin says it lasted about five seconds. And it just started again. But my whole life stopped at that point. And then when it was over, I got on stage and you have to do a Q and A. A couple of polite people said, 'Oh, well done,' then gave me their business card. And to be honest it ends up being the biggest anti-climax in the world, because all your life you want to make films and everything is 'One day I'll get to make a film' and you finally get to make one and you finally show it and then you get a couple of business cards. And that's the end of the night. And*

initially you think, 'Why did I do this? It's twenty years of trying to do this, just for what?'"

— Gareth Edwards

For two decades Gareth had strived and strived to get to this point and now this is the disappointing result. His world had come crashing down. However, that gut-wrenching feeling of disappointment would be short-lived.

"Then I got really lucky. One of those business cards was from a gentleman who, the next day, found me. I had to do an interview for a website that no one would have ever heard of and after it was over, this guy comes up and he says, 'Oh hi. My name is Mike Simpson. I was at the screening last night, I gave you my card,' and I was like, 'Oh yeah I'm really sorry, I was going to call you.' He went, 'Do you have a moment? I'd like to talk to you.' So then he starts saying, 'I'm from Hollywood and I represent directors and I just deal with directors.' After he asked a few questions, he said, 'I'd love to represent you.' And I was just thinking 'Yeah' and then he goes, 'Don't you want to know who else I represent?' and he said: 'Quentin Tarantino, Tim Burton, people like Wes Craven and John Woo,' and I was like, 'You want to represent me?' And then I thought, 'OK, I know how this is going to work: you say this and then I never see you again. Right?' But it wasn't like that."

— Gareth Edwards

This was the turning point. Everything changed from that moment. *Monsters* was then shown in L.A. and movie producers were invited to come and see it. And Gareth had to introduce the film to the audience.

> *"I go in and I'm like, 'Hi I'm Gareth, from England. I made this film, did the visual effects myself and it was a very small crew,' and as I'm saying this I'm just looking at the crowd and there's Quentin Tarantino in the audience and I'm going, 'Ah ****!' I say all this stuff and then I leave and I get really nervous, you know; my heroes are watching this film."*
> – Gareth Edwards

And then after the film, Gareth gets to meet Tarantino.

> *"Someone must've told him I was a massive fan. I must have seen 'Reservoir Dogs' seven times at the cinema, I loved it. And he came over. And he starts talking to me, and you know when you're like, 'OK remember this Gareth. Remember everything he says. This is it. This will never happen again.' And all I'm thinking the whole time is like, 'Oh My God, it's Quentin Tarantino.' He's going 'Waa waa waa waa.' The subtitles just go: 'I'm Quentin Tarantino and I'm talking to you, right now.' And then he left and everyone comes over and said, 'What did he say?' And I was like, 'I have no idea'."*
> – Gareth Edwards

Hollywood found Gareth impressive, most impressive. Everyone wanted to get to know the Brit who'd wowed the filmmaking stalwarts of Tinseltown. For Gareth it was a whirlwind of going to studio after studio.

> *"In the space of two weeks I ended up meeting a hundred people. It was like crazy, they call it the 'water bottle tour,' where you sit in an office and you sort of meet usually two people, the Senior and Junior. And the junior person is really interested and engaged and saw the film and liked it and the senior person maybe saw it, maybe didn't, and he's usually on his Blackberry, going 'Uh-huh, uh-huh' and not really listening. And so did all that and a lot of it was a waste of time but there was a handful of meetings that felt really genuine and good. And one of them was with the movie company, Legendary, who ended up doing 'Godzilla'. And so they said, 'What are you doing the rest of the week?' and I was like, 'I've just got a whole load more meetings' and they went, 'Cancel them, you don't need to do them, you're going to make all your films with us from now on.' I was so taken aback I started crying and I was like, 'I'm sorry, you've got to talk amongst yourselves for a sec. I've waited all my life for someone like you to say something like that to me. And even if it's not true, like it just means a lot.' And he stuck to his word. Legendary, got me to direct 'Godzilla' and it was crazy!"*
>
> *– Gareth Edwards*

So, from one end of the spectrum to the other. The budget on *Monsters* had been chicken feed compared to the one he'd been given for the latest reboot of *Godzilla*. As his close friend Colin Goudie remembers:

> *"He went from the smallest budget movie of one hundred thousand dollars, which I think was the shooting budget on 'Monsters', to 'Godzilla', which I think the budget on that*

was one hundred and sixty million! And that's the biggest leap of any director in film history, to go from such a small budget to such a big budget!"

— Colin Goudie

Gareth's star was definitely on the rise. From stacking shelves in a supermarket to TV 'disaster porn' and now this. A multi-million-pound budget to direct a Hollywood blockbuster. Globally, *Godzilla* topped five hundred million dollars at the box office. Not bad for the boy from Nuneaton, whose love of film had come from wearing out an old Betamax copy of *Star Wars*. Gareth's dream of making films had come true, but his career was really about to make the jump into hyperspace.

"You should never really expect to have anything to do with 'Star Wars'. I thought George was going to retire and that was just going to be episode one to six and that is it. And that maybe decades from now someone might consider, 'Shall we try and do the end trilogy?' I didn't expect it to happen in my lifetime, like in terms of my career. And I definitely didn't expect to be offered one of them. But at some point they said, 'If you're ever free, no rush, you know, pop in and say hello.' But I didn't make myself free at that point. About a year went by, because J.J. Abrams was doing Episode 7 and I didn't know what their timeline was. I don't know what they want to talk about. Maybe they're going to do a TV show or something? So, whilst I was finishing 'Godzilla', Warner Brothers is right next to Disney, so I could sneak out and I quickly went out one afternoon and I saw Kiri Hart at Disney and we got on really well. We just talked to each other about why we love

'Star Wars', why we think it was a success. And I wasn't really auditioning for anything because I didn't want to do another big film. I was getting to the end of 'Godzilla' and I was exhausted and I wanted to do my own things. And then about a week later, I got an email that said, 'What do you think to these two documents?' and they came with passwords and I thought that when I typed the password in it would trigger them knowing that I'd read it. And I didn't have time to write a proper response that was articulate until the weekend. And I didn't want to look like I'd read it and hadn't got back to them. So I actually didn't open them for about four or five days until I had a Sunday off, where I could read them and write something sensible back."

— Gareth Edwards

What Gareth didn't know at this point was that he had the passwords to a document that every *Star Wars* fan in the world would give almost anything for. This was the very beginning of *Rogue One: A Star Wars Story*. Having put off opening them, Gareth eventually typed in the password, that would unlock a whole new project for him.

"I opened it and started reading it and it's only when I got to the end that I started to realise: 'Hang on a minute, this is connecting directly with the original 'New Hope' and they're going to make a film that's the direct prequel to 'Star Wars'! That's sacrilegious. You shouldn't do that. You can't make that movie. What if it's anything less than brilliant? That's wrong'. And I then started to think, 'Hang on a minute, am I being offered this? Is this something they're going to do and they want me to be part of it? Because how can you say no?' It was sort of this weird checkmate, where you

think you shouldn't do this, but you're also like…you can't not do it. The idea of whatever years later, you would see it at the cinema and it ends and someone else's name comes up. And you think, 'I could've done that.' What else, why are you alive if you're not going to take these sorts of risks? The thing I spent the most time thinking about as a kid was 'Star Wars' and fantasizing about that world. And so when someone says to you, 'How about making a 'Star Wars' movie?' You half go 'Whoa! Oh I don't know if I want to do that. That's a lot of pressure.' Then the other part of you goes: 'Wait a minute, if you were going to do anything, if you want to be a filmmaker and you love 'Star Wars', you should make a 'Star Wars' film, right?' And you go, 'Wait, it doesn't work like that, there's a lot of pressure, and everyone has an opinion' and they're like, 'No, but come on Gareth you want to be a filmmaker, you love 'Star Wars', this is a no- brainer!' And you start going, 'Oh yeah, I guess it's a no-brainer. I guess I should do it'. But I thought they'd sent it to about ten different filmmakers and I was one of them. And they were just seeing what everyone had to say about it. Then the more I went in for meetings and the more I met with them, the more I started to realise, 'Hang on, I don't think they're talking to anyone else.' And I thought it was like maybe eight years from now, I didn't know it was going to be next. As soon as 'Godzilla' was finished, I basically got this message, like 'OK, we're going to do 'Rogue One' next, you'd better get to San Francisco', so I had ten days off in between 'Godzilla' and 'Rogue One'."

– *Gareth Edwards*

The road ahead would certainly not be an easy one for Gareth. He would be working with some of the best filmmakers in the world at LucasFilm and working with some of the most precious intellectual property on planet Earth. Who better to have in the cutting room than an old friend? Colin Goudie was about to be reunited with his sci-fi chum.

> *"You never forget the day you get the 'Star Wars' phone call. So, the phone rings. I'd had surgery, I was upstairs in my house. I can hear the phone ringing and I'm trying to get down the stairs without ending up back in hospital for more surgery and of course the answer phone clicks in. And this voice is leaving this message and I'm now thinking, 'Oh my gosh,' so I picked up the phone. 'Hello?' Pippa Anderson the Head of Post-Production at LucasFilm calling. She wanted to talk to me about coming onboard with 'Rogue One'. And would I be interested? Was I available? And she'd been told by Gareth I was recovering from surgery and I couldn't go to Pinewood straight away. But they set up a meeting with me and they waited for me, which was incredible. So four weeks later I was able to drive again and I drove down to Pinewood and I had a meeting. And they just wanted to talk to me about the process I'd worked with Gareth on 'Monsters'. They explain basically there are going to be other editors, effectively an editor they want, a studio editor. Somebody who had worked on a two-hundred-million-dollar movie before, which I certainly hadn't!"*
>
> *– Colin Goudie*

So, initially, Colin was brought onboard, not to edit the movie, but to help put the story of *Rogue One* together. To storyboard the idea, which would, in turn, assist in getting the movie made.

> *"What they wanted from me to start with, before any of the rest of the process was underway, was Gareth wanted to*

make a story reel. So the story reel is something that's becoming a lot more common on big movies now, whereby you make the film, before you make the film! And in this sense what Gareth wanted me to do was to rip hundreds of movies and piece together the story, because we didn't have a screenplay at that point, so he could see how long action sequences would last before going to the next dialogue scene; how long the dialogue scene should last before going back to the next action scene. It's one of those things that if you write on the page 'An Imperial shuttle lands on the planet,' that takes maybe three seconds to read. But if you go and watch a 'Star Wars' film, if you watch 'Return of the Jedi', it takes maybe thirty or forty seconds for that to happen. So I was ripping, obviously, the 'Star Wars' films, but other science fiction films, as well. Science fiction particularly uses very extended sequences of spaceships doing things. If you watch '2001' you think how minimalist the dialogue is in that film, how long it takes things to move, and even in the 'Star Wars' films it does that, too, before you get into the actual battle scenes. The opening of 'A New Hope', if you read that line it will say 'A Star Destroyer comes into frame.' But that shot goes on forever. And then there's the Blockade Runner, then there's a whole Star Destroyer that follows it. What Gareth didn't want to do was too many dialogue scenes being written by the writers and not enough room for expansive shots of ships and planets and storytelling, all of the visual things. That's what people want."

– *Colin Goudie*

Colin got to work on editing the reel in Britain; he felt there was no need for him to go to the States to do this. It would, after all, be a waste of money. But Gareth made him see the opportunities a trip to America might bring.

> *"I said to Gareth, 'There is no reason for me to travel to California to go to Lucasfilm to do this. You can save some money.' And he said, 'Yes, but if they meet you, they will fall in love with you, they'll want you to work on the whole film.' So, basically, this was an audition; cutting the story reel is my audition for Lucasfilm. Gareth's like, 'Yes, it is.' So I jumped on a plane to San Francisco, went to work at Lucasfilm and got to meet John Knoll, got to meet Dennis Muren, got to meet Doug Chiang, the production designer, and was really part of the team. Sure enough, at the end of those ten weeks I got called into the offices by the producers, they said, 'We'd actually like you to come onboard now and cut the pre-visualisation. That's going to take six months, then we'd like you to come on editorial and work on the movie itself.'"*
>
> *– Colin Goudie*

With Colin onboard *Rogue One*, it was like all of the planets had aligned for Gareth. His friend, whom he'd met in the edit corridors of the British Broadcasting Corporation, was with him on his greatest adventure! They had bonded over their love of science fiction and of *Star Wars*. And here they were, Colin who'd grown up in Rushden in Northamptonshire and Gareth from Nuneaton, working with the best of the best at LucasFilm. This movie would sit right before the original *Star Wars* began. So, as an ultimate fan of *Star Wars*, now in the director's chair, attention to detail would be everything for Gareth.

> *"If you were in the London area in 2015 and you had 1970s sideburns, you were guaranteed a part in Rogue One!"*
> – *Gareth Edwards*

CHAPTER ELEVEN
The First Spin-Off

(From interviews with
Film Editor: Colin Goudie
Director: Gareth Edwards)

THE RELEASE DATE for *Rogue One: A Star Wars Story* had been slated for December 2016. Principal photography for the movie would begin in the summer of 2015. But before all of that, a very excited couple of nerds from England were getting the guided tour of Skywalker Ranch in California. And they could raid the archives!

> *"Thankfully, 'Star Wars' is pretty well-documented, like with the archives and everything. George Lucas was really good at that. They kept a lot of things. When we went through the archives, we did this fanboy's dream of you get to hold Luke Skywalker's lightsaber, put on Han Solo's jacket, Darth Vader's mask, and all this sort of stuff. And it's amazing. And on the way out as you're going down to the basement, there are all these canisters of film on the wall and you go, 'What are they?' And they say, 'They're the negatives and the*

prints of all the dailies, all the footage from 'Star Wars'.' And you go, 'What everything?' And they go, 'Yeah. All the outtakes, everything!' 'Can we look at these?' 'Sure.' And then we ended up going back to the negative and getting the best version we could. And we were like, 'OK, we could use some of this in 'Rogue One'.' It would be great to have the pilots from the attack on the Death Star of 'A New Hope' in 'Rogue One' but not the same clips. Let's try and find other moments where they say different lines of dialogue or something and put them in.' Which is what ended up happening. So, we did all that."

– Gareth Edwards

Even though *Rogue One* wasn't billed as a prequel, it is of course the pre-cursor to the original film. You can basically start *A New Hope* as *Rogue One* ends and they could be one long movie. Gareth's challenge, among countless others, was to ensure that a 21st century movie had the feel of the 1970s.

"Obviously our bible and blueprint for everything was how they did the original. Let's try and copy and replicate that because of the crossover that was happening in our film. And the more you look at what they did back then, the more respect you ended up having for it. My God, they were so innovative with the resources they had! Even like building the Death Star, in the control room, where Grand Moff Tarkin is. They built only what they needed, in terms of the backgrounds. And they would reuse it and re-jiggle them to get another side on film."

– Gareth Edwards

The First Spin-Off

But not everything was well-documented and for some very important props they had to use their ingenuity.

"There were some things that weren't recorded. For instance, the Death Star plans. We couldn't find anywhere, any image ever, other than what's in the film of the card that Princess Leia puts into R2-D2. It doesn't exist. No one took a picture of it. So using the most high resolution scan of that, which is technically the Blu-ray really of 'A New Hope', we had to reverse engineer what was on there and it looked like there was this circular disk but it was also like a credit card and so the prop designers were really good, they came up with this whole thing like in a close-up would look good. So that worked. Then there's the guy who's on Yavin, the sentry, who's in the bucket on the tower. He's kind of got this scanner, whatever it is; it's like he's doing speeding fines for the ships! He's like, 'Yeah, you'll get a ticket in the post!' We didn't know what that was. Someone calls up the guy who shot that footage, and says, 'By any chance do you remember what that was? We haven't got any reference of it.' He said, 'I think it was a light meter.' We didn't have anything; we decided he should have something in his hand so we took a light meter, it was two light meters taped together. So then we try to find the light meters. No matter how we looked at them we couldn't really arrange them but we used it as the basis to create that device. We were trying to be as authentic as possible. The rules were, whatever they did on the original, that was what we were going to do. We are going to completely be true to that. But we've got high-definition cameras now and the detail is a little bit cleaner. So, for instance, the Rebel helmets

really just had a coat hanger wire coming out of the helmet. And you could tell on certain shots, with our cameras that would look bad. We had to invent little ends to the metal, we were seeing a little bit more detail in whatever you saw in the original. Even the Stormtrooper helmets, they've got this blue little grill down the side, that was just a sticker, back in the day. But it would look like a sticker on our cameras. So we had to create actual grooves and put a blue surface underneath. Everything based on what it was, but with much more detail."

– Gareth Edwards

Colin Goudie remembers very early on that his mate wanted *Rogue One* filmed traditionally, the way the very first *Star Wars* had been, in the roasting summer of 1976. But the new home of *Star Wars* in Britain, was Pinewood Studios.

"To get to go to Pinewood, which was just getting bigger and bigger, and we were building more stages and more and more sets, that was just incredible. And Gareth wanted practical sets, he didn't want massive amounts of green screen. So you were actually walking onto a set with real X-Wings, you can go over and touch the X-Wing. Don't break it! And the droids are all actually really moving around. Radio-controlled droids! And the aliens are all people in costumes. I remember when the costume tests came in, I got to edit all the costume tests together for lighting and things. It was mind-boggling!"

– Colin Goudie

The First Spin-Off

And, as a lifelong *Star Wars* fan, there were many mind-boggling moments for Colin!

> *"The weirdest experience was during the very early days on 'Rogue', on the pre-visualisation, and I was sitting in a meeting and there was a behind-the-scenes crew who were filming footage of the meeting, as it was going on. The head of Pre-Viz was there and his team. Gareth was there and I was the only person there from Editorial. And I was listening to these incredibly talented people talking about a scene that we were about to do and I suddenly realised that I wasn't watching the behind-the-scenes on a DVD. I was in a meeting and I had to contribute to that meeting. Oh yeah, they want my opinion. I'm not just here to watch. I'm here as the editor to say, 'I think I need this shot, I need that shot. Or would this be a better shot?' And suddenly, I'm like: 'Wow! I'm actually working on a 'Star Wars' film.' Going onto those sets, the sets they build at Pinewood are just incredible. And you go on, and it's all these British crews and they've worked on all the big Bond films and the 'Star Wars' films and Marvel films. You're walking onto a 'Star Wars' set, just surrounded by all this British talent and you do feel incredibly proud when you're on that set, I have to say!"*
>
> *– Colin Goudie*

Another aspect that was very important to the director, Gareth Edwards, was shooting at an original location. Cardington Studios in Bedfordshire would welcome *Star Wars* once again, just as it had done in the 1970s.

> "I became a sucker for anything that was the original movie, so we knew we had to build Yavin and the hangar for the Rebels. We looked at different locations and there were all these different ones, then finally we went to this place in Cardington, in Bedfordshire, and when we were stood there someone said, 'By the way do you know this is the exact spot where C-3PO and R2-D2 and Princess Leia and Han Solo were stood for that shot, that exterior shot, like punctuation moment before the briefing of the attack on the Death Star?' And then it was like, 'Well we're definitely filming it here, right? Why wouldn't you film it here? Like this is where Yavin was. Why didn't we come here first?' Back in the day what they did, I think it was actually doubles, it wasn't really Harrison and Mark and Anthony Daniels, it was doubles I think, that were in that shot. And then they did the matte painting of the hangar, so we were actually in the very same space and created that hangar for real. And we could go in and it was probably the biggest set we built. And I'm sure it cost a lot of money!"
>
> – Gareth Edwards

Gareth remembers that getting everything just right was a huge team effort, across all of the departments who were working on *Rogue One*.

> "Hats off to our costume department, because we knew we were going to have Darth Vader in the film and if you look at all the original Vader masks and the way they did them, the very first Vader mask was sculpted out of clay. And as a result there are slight fingerprints and not perfect lines,

The First Spin-Off

very slight imperfections throughout. Now on the computer you can solve all that and make it perfect. The initial pass of Vader's helmet in the computer that was going to be 3-D printed, was way too perfect. And didn't look like Vader. So we had to go and look at the original mask and slightly warp it and make it look a bit more organic. We even put little thumbprints in it. So it had all the imperfections of 1977. You can't see it when you look at it, but if you don't do it, it looks wrong. It's like, 'Something's up, this isn't really Vader.' And everything was a bit like that, where you just knew as a kid because you'd watched it so many times; you just know if it was 'Star Wars' or not. It's this vocabulary that got established that I love. To me it's like the perfect aesthetic. Normally when you work on a film, you find yourself going, 'You can't do that, because it's too much like 'Star Wars'.' This was the time we can do it! We've got to do it. We can make it like 'Star Wars', this isn't going to happen again. This is the only time in your life. You can go for what you want and have it look just like 'Star Wars'. Hopefully identical. Even the guns I'd never really studied, I never knew there was going to be a test. Like when you watched 'Star Wars' as a kid and then you end up in these situations where the props department are laying out all of these guns and going, 'Here are some guns ideas for 'Rogue One'.' And they lay them out. They had what felt like thirty or forty, and I'm going through them all and sort of pick one up and I go, 'This is a bit too much just like something from World War II and it doesn't feel like 'Star Wars'.' And then they go, 'That's exactly the gun the Stormtroopers have in Mos Eisley,' or whatever, and you'd go, 'Er, OK, this is perfect!' And you start to realise that 'Star Wars' is just fifteen percent sci-fi but mostly history. It's not as futuristic as you think, because in your brain it's spaceships, you think all sci-fi, but actually the majority of the costumes and the props have something that's very much stolen, because they had to. They were borrowing from the aesthetic of World War II and the past, even biblical settings; the fact they shot in North Africa. I think that really helped because that made it like a story from the Bible and gave it that mythological, ancient feel. But, if for some reason they had picked a different setting, I'm not sure it would have been the same."

— Gareth Edwards

You'd think most directors would be intimidated with shooting a *Star Wars* movie, but when it came to filming, Gareth being such a fan, felt right at home.

"It's weird. It was like what the brochure promised as a kid. 'Life is going to be spaceships, robots, explosions, planets, princesses and lightsabers. That's what life will be.' And then you hit this point when you go, 'Wait a minute, no it's not, this is a lie and all my toys aren't real and these places don't exist.' And coming to terms with what real life is, it's not that thing they promised on the screen, it's actually a lot more boring than that, was kind of like the big adjustment. And then when you get to do 'Star Wars', everyone was like, 'Oh my God! Was it crazy?' and I'd say, 'No, it was really kind of normal.' Because it was what was promised in the brochure. When we were kids they always said we'd be hanging out around X-Wings and next to Stormtroopers, that's what we

> were told as kids. It's what life was. And it was going back to what you thought life would be. And you go, 'Yay! OK good! Finally!' And I felt comfortable in that sense. It's like a comfort blanket. If you needed to be as cosy as you could possibly be, you'd probably want to go back to your place of childhood. And see those things, those images, and be in that place that you grew up in. That's where most people feel relaxed and comfortable and 'Star Wars' is that place for me and a lot of other people. So, weirdly, standing on a set next to an X-Wing and everything else, it's like this calming thing where you go, you just feel back home, back in that safe place of being young. You can't get stressed out next to a Stormtrooper. It just feels right. It's everything else that's wrong."
>
> – Gareth Edwards

While Gareth was getting to relive his childhood on the sets and working long hours shooting the movie, Film Editor Colin Goudie was back in the edit suite, ploughing through the dailies as they came in.

> "Gareth, as the filmmaker, likes to have actors run with the flow and do improvisation. So Gareth will do a take and can sometimes run that camera for an hour. 'And reset.' And maybe they will run back to first positions, or just carry on. What he wants from that is a moment of truth, he calls it. He's always looking for the moment of truth and I think Stanley Kubrick would do it by doing one hundred and six takes, the legendary Kubrick method. Gareth's is, 'You do one take, and it lasts one hundred and six minutes!' And you have to go through it all and find that moment of truth!

> *And they were long days, some of them twenty hours, some of them twenty-four hour, but every single day was, 'Pinch me, I'm working on a 'Star Wars' film'. And my edit desk at work used to be covered with my 'Star Wars' collection of memorabilia, that I've been buying since 1977. My little Millennium Falcon, that I bought back then. My lightsaber, all these things were all over the desk. People would come in, like Kathy Kennedy, and say, 'This is such a fun room.' There were like blasters everywhere, and lightsabers. People just liked that environment. Some edit suites seem to be very clinical and clean. Some editors like a very de-cluttered working environment so they can just focus on what's on the screen. My edit suite is the opposite, the anti-universe to that. My edit suite is like the toy store Hamleys."*
>
> *– Colin Goudie*

Colin says having all of his *Star Wars* toys populating his working area was a real inspiration and helped to fuel the editing process.

> *"It genuinely helps you with the creative process. Because I would be cutting a scene in the film and I'd be thinking, 'Do you know, I want a shot of a Stormtrooper falling off of a platform.' And I would reach for my 12-inch Stormtrooper figure and I had a blue wall in my edit suite. And I would photograph it falling and do various shots and then I could copy that into part of the shot. I could send that off to Pre-Viz and say, 'Can you pre-viz that up for me?' And they would match the shot. And they'd do it properly and send that to set and say pick that shot up. It was a toyshop and everything in that room got used at some point or another. Other people*

The First Spin-Off

would come in and photograph them. One of the concept artists, Duncan Fegrado, would actually sit next to me, he would set his workstation up next to me and he would constantly be drawing my Stormtroopers. He would say, 'What's this shot you need of Jyn or Cassian putting the blaster away, what's the close-up you need?' And he would take my blaster and he'd photograph it and he'd go and draw it. At one point I remember building Scarif in my edit suite and putting AT-ATs and tanks and towers and all sorts of things with the toys, and working out blocking and camera angles. And getting people in, getting the concept artists and the Pre-Viz people and showing them and explaining to them where we felt Jyn and Cassian would be going from this part of the island to that part of the island. We weren't starting with a blank canvas. It's much easier to explain to somebody design if you have physically got something in front of you."

– Colin Goudie

While shooting *Rogue One*, it became apparent to Director Gareth Edwards that he was working with *Star Wars* pedigree. Just as *Star Wars* is about the Skywalker bloodline, it appeared that the galaxy ran in the blood of some of the crew as well.

"The second assistant director is called Andy, his job on 'Rogue One' was to shoot a lot of the pilots, X-Wing pilot footage. He would set up the shots, we'd talk it through with the actors in the morning, but then for the rest of the day he'd be left alone and he'd be doing all the directions like, 'OK, look left. Turn hard right. Fire!' You know and say the line. And I was like that's a cool job for the day; one day he was like, 'You know

what, Gareth? This is really strange because my dad was the AD on 'A New Hope' and he did this exact same thing, he shot the X-Wing pilots.' Wow! And so then it felt like we are benefitting from generations of experience being handed down. I am pulling from all my favourite films as well, to try to make this movie, and two of my favourite films are 'Alien' and 'Aliens', and this planet Eadu in our movie, which is a rainy planet, I said to Neil Lamont, who's our production designer, 'I want it to look like 'Aliens'. I want it to feel like that kind of storm planet.' And Neil sort of smiled. He says, 'My dad was the production designer on that.' So he knew all the tricks and how to make that set exactly right. Also, how to do the lighting and the way it was hazed up and the silhouette kind of shapes. He had some behind-the-scenes pictures from 'Aliens'! There's like this family, like a travelling circus, I guess, that sort of exists on the outskirts of London, where there are these generations of different people who've passed down all these tricks of the trade. We benefitted as well from 'The Force Awakens'. Obviously the success of that film, but from the fact that they had to set up this kind of 'Star Wars' factory to make all these things. They learned how to do it by the time they got to the end of 'The Force Awakens', so when we came in with 'Rogue One' it was very efficient."

– Gareth Edwards

And even in post-production, Gareth was still making sure this would have a feel of *A New Hope* from 1977.

"We degraded it, we put grain in. We were as keen to make it look like the seventies as possible, even a little undulation,

The First Spin-Off

like you get with projected footage, where it just slightly undulates, things like this. There were just little things we did, for certain shots. We didn't want it to feel like digital, we wanted to make it to look like it was footage that we'd found from the seventies."

– Gareth Edwards

As someone who'd initially been brought on to the film just to cut the mood reel, Colin Goudie was now a part of the furniture at LucasFilm.

"I was on it for 27 months in total! I ended up getting a shared credit with Jabez Olsen and John Gilroy. The scenes that I loved cutting were the ones on the beach in the sunset, at the end, between Jyn and Cassian. Gareth actually filmed that on three consecutive nights, because of the sun setting. You can only film for a very limited period of time, to get those shots. I used pieces from each of the takes they'd shot. I actually finished that at four o'clock in the morning."

– Colin Goudie

And the completion of *Rogue One: A Star Wars Story* was right up to the wire. Colin Goudie was burning the midnight oil.

"When you are working on films, on 'film', the way that they would have back in 1976 and 1977 for the release, you have to finish months in advance to physically make the hundreds of prints that are going to the cinema. Whereas we were still tinkering with 'Rogue One' right into December, and you are tinkering with things right up until the last minute. I was over at IMAX doing the IMAX prints and John Gilroy was

tinkering with things back in San Francisco and supervising the mix. Everything was going right up to the wire. At this point, it's very close to the movie's release time! I was aware as a fan how disappointed people are with films that have got a fan-base. So I came onto that movie wanting 'Rogue One' to be a film that I would want to go and see. At the end I was screening the film I think at IMAX, three times a day, checking the print. So when you sit through that movie three times in a single day and you still enjoy it, I think I've hit the target working on a film that we're all so proud of and that is going to appeal to the fans, as well as people who had never seen a 'Star Wars' movie before. I think 'Rogue' ticked both those boxes. I was very pleased about that."

– *Colin Goudie*

Gareth remembers the moment when he had to readjust to the real world and that moment of truth when everyone would get to see *Rogue One*.

"You don't realise just how affected you are. You have to cut an emotional cord when you are making a film. It's such a rollercoaster. If you look online, people's reactions are so extreme that if you genuinely feel everything, every little molecule of what everyone is thinking, you are going to have a nervous breakdown, or something. So you have to cut the cord. You have to in order to survive this process. And so you do that and then right at the very end, you've got like a week where are you are surgically trying to reconnect that cord. So you can enjoy it. Because you become this numb sort of machine, to get through the making of the film. Then sud-

The First Spin-Off

denly it starts unfolding, when posters start turning up on billboards and you don't quite believe this, this is not real. It's really hard to quickly change gear and feel it and let it hit you. It was really surreal because when we did 'Rogue One' everything is very surrounded in secrecy. As the film began, you think, 'What if everyone hates this, what if it isn't liked by anybody?' But thank God we're in America, because they're quite vocal. And you start to hear reactions, which did make us feel better. It was probably one of the best experiences I've ever had. By the end of the movie, it just felt so good and just a relief that people didn't hate it. That was my biggest fear, the whole time. I didn't want to be that guy that people shouted at across the street, saying: 'You ruined my childhood.' But for me, when it ends, and it says 'Directed by Gareth Edwards' it is weird, with that iris wipe. I watched those credits on 'Star Wars' probably more than any film as a kid and that's how it felt like the ultimate film ends. I guess when that happened on the premiere it did feel like, 'Ok I can die now. Whatever happens the rest of my life, I've done that. I can die!'"

– *Gareth Edwards*

CHAPTER TWELVE
The British Force

(From interviews with
Production Supervisor: Robert Watts
Producer: Gary Kurtz
20th Century Fox Executive: Peter Beale
Set Decorator: Roger Christian
Assistant Art Director: Les Dilley
Costume Designer: John Mollo
Creature Maker: Nick Maley
Film Editor: Colin Goudie
Director: Gareth Edwards)

ROGUE ONE: *A Star Wars Story* was the eighth movie in the franchise. It stormed the box office and was a massive hit. The long relationship of *Star Wars* and Britain is still flourishing to this day, but it all started back in the 1970s. So what is it that makes shooting in the UK so special? The filmmakers have their own ideas. *Rogue One* Director Gareth Edwards:

> "It's something to do with the British personality. It shouldn't count for anything but it really does. It's like, everyone's really nice and very modest, friendly and humble. And nothing is a problem, they never say no. We used to joke we would say 'you can say no. Just say no you can't do it'. And they wouldn't do it. They'd be like, 'Let me look into it. I'll come back to you.' And they will always come back with a solution. They pride themselves on never letting you down. All the characters are so sweet, it was just a great experience in terms of the crew and everybody who worked on it. I think it would be very easy to argue you work with the best in the world!"
>
> – Gareth Edwards

And for *Rogue One* Film Editor Colin Goudie it's all about the pride he feels in being part of that British movie legacy.

> "I know that I'm personally so proud to be a Brit working on a 'Star Wars' movie and I know that all the other Brits working on it as well feel the same. I was pretty much the old man on the crew. Most people on the film were twenty years younger than me, so they had actually grown up with 'Star Wars'. They'd seen the 'Star Wars' movies on DVD or VHS the first time; they have not had the cinema experience. So, for them to be working on movies they have gone into, that being a lifetime's ambition. For me it was an ambition from the age of sixteen, for them it was from the age of three. You're aware that these are the biggest movies in the world. You've got 'Star Wars' and you've got 'Harry Potter'. These are the movies that the whole world is going to watch. And they're made in Britain! The line from 'Star Wars' that stuck

in my head the most, in 1977, is to do with being a farm boy. If there is a bright centre to the universe, this is the spot it's farthest from. And growing up where I grew up, in the middle of nowhere, a hike to get to the nearest town, to get to the cinema showing 'Star Wars', was a huge distance, not like today. To go from that childhood to ending up walking on a set, you know standing next to an X-Wing, I feel like I have arrived at the centre of the universe!"

– Colin Goudie

After *The Empire Strikes Back*, Producer Gary Kurtz and George Lucas went their separate ways. And Gary went from working with Yoda to a whole new universe of puppets!

"Well, after 'Empire Strikes Back' I was pressured by Jim Henson, because we had agreed to do the 'The Dark Crystal' together; he'd been working on it for several years before that. George wanted to change the script of 'Return of the Jedi' significantly. I felt I would rather have a newer challenge, a different kind of film. And 'The Dark Crystal' was certainly that. It's been the only large-scale major studio film that doesn't have any human beings in it. It is all mechanical creatures. And it was all made in the days before CGI. There was no chance to create anything artificially through computer animation, so it was a really interesting challenge; it took a long time to do and again it was a unique film and I really enjoyed working on it."

– Gary Kurtz

Star Wars brought Gary from the States to the UK for filming, but he ended up making London his home.

> *"I decided it was just easier to work here because low-budget financing was easier and there were more interesting films made in the UK and the rest of Europe than were being made in Hollywood at that time. The eighties, the end of the eighties and into the nineties were kind of a bad time in the Hollywood industry and then it got better again. So it was just a decision that was based on that."*
>
> *– Gary Kurtz*

But for Gary, like many of the others, it was *Star Wars* that really got the filmmaking ball rolling.

> *"I'm incredibly proud. I think that all of the effort that we put in, trying to get the film off the ground and getting it made paid off really well. It's always a big plus to be involved with a film that turns out to be a big hit. I wouldn't trade it for anything."*
>
> *– Gary Kurtz*

And 20th Century Fox Executive Peter Beale remembers how *Star Wars*, becoming that big hit, really turned things around.

> *"It revitalised 20th Century Fox and it revitalised England. Because the studios started to see that we were making, good films, cheaply! And it brought work back to England."*
>
> *– Peter Beale*

The British Force

Peter had worked very closely with Gary Kurtz and George Lucas. He went on to have a very successful career in Hollywood. For many years, he lived a stone's throw from the iconic Fox building in Los Angeles. But in his opinion, *Star Wars* could have only been made in Britain.

> *"The studios in America had become very solid and very conservative. The heads of production of all the big studios had turned the film down and I just don't think they were mentally open to try all these new things. We in Britain had no work. We had wonderful crews, you look at the crews the British have. We have this combination of creativity, hard work and skills sort of, almost a military skill, and so I think that would have been impossible to have been made in America at the time. And what the British crews, the English actors brought was something that couldn't be got anywhere else and I still think the first 'Star Wars' is the best one. It's got this magic about it. I am proud, but I don't have pride. I don't know how you'd say it. I loved doing it, but I don't go around talking about it. It's part of the things we've done. I'm very pleased to have been part of a team and, in fact, put the team together. And in a way quietly steered them. So yes, proud from that point of view."*
> – Peter Beale

Peter and his wife Francesca have now left L.A. and moved to Spain. Peter is far from retired; immersing himself in lectures, documentaries, writing and environmental projects.

Art Director Les Dilley moved up the ranks and became a production designer, basing himself in Los Angeles during his long career in film.

"I've been in the business for sixty years. It's the excitement of it all, it's never been boring, I've never had a boring job. And it was 'Star Wars' that propelled me. Without question! It did."

– Les Dilley

Les has now retired. His very last job was working on a BBC children's series called *Tea Cup Travels,* as the production designer. Les and his wife now spend some of their leisure time in Baja, the very place where his career started to take off, on the movie *Lucky Lady*. Almost perfect symmetry.

Having strived for so long to be recognised, 'creature maker' Nick Maley's career began to take off for him after *The Empire Strikes Back*. A certain small green alien had certainly helped with that.

"Yoda was very special to me; he changed my life and so I really couldn't possibly say there was another creature that I was involved with that I have the same fondness for."

– Nick Maley

Nick doesn't work in the movie industry now, but is far from retired. Along with his wife, he runs a museum based on the movies, on the paradise island of Saint Maarten.

"I just like the Caribbean. I had been doing some movies that were really extraordinarily tough. One was 'The Keep', which was like a prison sentence. And the second one was 'Highlander', which was a great movie but I had a number of political issues with the cinematographer and some other people who really didn't think a guy with a make-up ticket should be telling the cameraman to turn the camera over, because I was trying to direct the second unit. I

had already done it on 'Lifeforce' but when I tried to do it on 'Highlander' I met with a lot of resistance. You go from that to sitting on a sandy beach, with a piña colada in your hand, under an umbrella, with the sea lapping against your toes and you're thinking, 'Why am I working ninety-six hours a week? In a dirty workshop?' The truth of the matter is when you've worked on fifty-three of fifty-four movies, fifty-five doesn't really make a difference! I believe that life is about having those broad experiences. Experiencing as much as possible. I'm very lucky. I started out as the kid who had nothing, in low-income housing. I went through the period of struggling to realise my dreams. I went through the period of making movies and creating images that no one could have imagined. Now, I'm still doing conventions and running a museum and encouraging kids to follow their dreams. It's been a great ride. And it's not over yet. Life is good. 'Star Wars' has given me everything!"

– Nick Maley

After *The Empire Strikes Back*, costume designer John Mollo won his second Academy Award for his work on the 1982 movie *Gandhi*. Having delved into the world of science-fiction with *Star Wars*, John would find himself in more familiar territory. Given his background of military history, he was ideal to give authenticity to the British TV series *Sharpe*, a fictional character set in the Napoleonic wars, portrayed by actor Sean Bean.

John Mollo's final foray into science fiction came with the 1997 movie *Event Horizon*.

Looking back on *Star Wars*, John remembers it for the great collaboration between Britain and America.

> *"George Lucas got the job done, with a bit of help! It was a galaxy Britain built!"*
>
> *– John Mollo*

John Mollo passed away in October 2017. His contribution to film history is unquestionable. Some of his original artwork, in the making of *Star Wars*, went up for auction at Bonhams in London, in December 2018. His sketchbook, with designs from *A New Hope* and *The Empire Strikes Back*, sold for one hundred thousand pounds. Tom Mollo, John's son, fondly remembers how his late father's talents all came together in the creative process.

> *"I think it was the combination of his military knowledge (of how uniforms and equipment should work), his obsession with authenticity and his natural artistic ability that made his work on 'Star Wars' such a success. Ultimately, we all believed in the characters because their clothes and kit looked real and so we thought the characters were real!"*
>
> *– Tom Mollo*

Set Decorator Roger Christian lives in Toronto, in Canada, and is still working in the movie industry. After wrapping on principal photography on *The Empire Strikes Back*, Roger fondly remembers George Lucas helping him realise his dream to make his own movie, as a director.

> *"I'd written this epic that I couldn't afford to make at film school. George's thank you to me was he commissioned it to go out with 'The Empire Strikes Back'; that got me started as a director. So, I suddenly was in this position with this*

The British Force

epic called 'Black Angel', a mediaeval myth, with no money really, twenty-five thousand pounds, which was a grant. Anyway, we shot it in Scotland and the short film went out with 'The Empire Strikes Back', thanks to George!"

— Roger Christian

Roger is now in a position to make *Black Angel* into a feature length film. It's taken decades to get to this point.

"It's ready now. Everything is done and prepared. I wrote it really around one knight. I've now got a two-hour feature. The whole plot point was how he was resurrected and fights the black angel. He has to defeat the darkness. I was talking with George about it the last time I went to Skywalker Ranch, it's part of his history. And he said, 'I'm going to give you a piece of advice.' He said, 'Don't do what I did, get huge and big. Keep it very simple with a few characters and you connect to them like the first 'Star Wars'' and I said, 'That's exactly what I've written.' I always say to people, 'Don't let anybody tell you, you can't when you can!'"

— Roger Christian

All of the behind-the-scenes talent share the same mantra, believing in one's self and never, ever giving up. Maybe George Lucas himself had set the example of going above and beyond, inspiring those around him, convincing them he could do it.

Rogue One Director and lifelong *Star Wars* fan, Gareth Edwards, explains how he thinks George Lucas really tapped into popular culture.

"As a child, I couldn't have told you why I liked it. It was just like, 'It's obvious, right? It's 'Star Wars', it's amazing!' As an adult, or as a filmmaker, you sort of try and analyse these things and try and figure it out. When you get into making films, you start to think, 'What is a story? What makes a good story? What the hell are stories? What's going on here?' And I think one of the main reasons is that, as we reproduce, over generations, over thousands and thousands of years, we can kind of like recreate ourselves. But the thing that doesn't get recreated is the experience we've had, and so like the body is hardware and stories are the software that you load into the child, and the stories that we want to gravitate to we want to hear. It's a story about the boy who is a bit older than me, who went over the hill and had this adventure and he somehow got rid of the bad guy, and got the girl and came back to the village with this reward. And made life better. We all gravitate towards those kinds of stories, because the myth is more important than the reality. And I feel now at forty-one, I still feel that way. I still feel like 'Star Wars' is the best film ever made. I would argue that it was the greatest leap from what was before it to after it. It changed popular cinema more than anything else. And from the outside it looks like you're interested in robots and spaceships. But really there is this sort of religion, a religious side to 'Star Wars', a way of believing that you can achieve anything you want, if you just trust your instincts."

– Gareth Edwards

Gareth Edwards has very much been instrumental in expanding the galaxy and continuing the creator's vision, even though *Star Wars* may not always be showered with awards.

The British Force

"The success of 'Star Wars' is not measured by the box office, or what critics say when it comes out. I think the success of 'Star Wars' is measured thirty years from now when you're walking along the street and if you see a kid or an old guy wearing a T-shirt and he's got something from your movie on it, then you know you did OK. And those original British guys did more than OK. They were pretty incredible. If I'm honest, if I was working on that movie and you read that screenplay and you didn't know George Lucas and you hadn't seen maybe the concept art, you might go, 'What the hell is this? This sounds stupid.' In any other hands, it's a terrible movie. But in George Lucas's hands and the crew that came together around him, they made a masterpiece. You could easily see a version of that, that is terrible. And a lot of people tried to copy George Lucas afterwards and made terrible movies, to prove that fact."

– Gareth Edwards

Robert Watts, the production supervisor on *Star Wars*, spent the best part of fifteen years working with George Lucas. Robert was integral to two of the biggest movie franchises in history: *Star Wars* and *Indiana Jones*, earning producer credits on *Return of the Jedi*, *The Temple of Doom* and *The Last Crusade*. Robert feels privileged to have worked with such dedicated filmmakers in the UK.

"Here in Britain we have extraordinary talent, both in the acting profession but also, very importantly, in the production departments. We have extraordinarily talented production people, who can do more or less anything. You've only got to look at what's being made here, look at it, all of these

amazing films. I'm extremely proud to have been involved in it. I never at the time thought what would happen, but now after all these years, as I look at myself now as I get older, I think, 'Bloody hell Robert! How did that happen? It was something else!' To this very day, I still have to pinch myself because people say to me sometimes, 'You worked on 'Star Wars'!' When I went on to the set of 'The Force Awakens', for example, all of the crew, who were little children when the first film opened, were all coming up to see me and Norman Reynolds. And they were saying, 'Oh, you're legends!' I said, 'What are you talking about?' We did our job. You get viewed like that, but you don't feel like that. I don't feel like a legend. I was at a science fiction convention. I went there with some friends. I wasn't doing talks or anything like that. I met one guy there, he came up to me and he said, 'Thank you for my childhood.' And I almost burst into tears. It was very moving. But basically, it was George Lucas. And we were the ones who surrounded him, to help him get this onto the screen."

– Robert Watts

And the final word has to go to Producer Gary Kurtz, the one American in this part of the story. George Lucas's right hand man, who himself traded in the warm, sunny climes of California for London. The producer who helped keep the movie on track and motivate the Brits behind the galaxy, something that continues to this day, with the latest *Star Wars* films.

The British Force

"They are entertaining and fun, which is the main thing we started with the original 'Star Wars' films. I've been pleased to see those, that they have continued that tradition well. And, of course, still with that British connection, something we started off in the seventies and I like that!"

– Gary Kurtz

About the Author

DAVID WHITELEY IS a British TV presenter and filmmaker. Born on May the Fourth (Yes, Star Wars day!), 1977 (the year Star Wars was released), he was destined to be a life-long fan of the movies. Having hit upon the idea of making a documentary about the Brits behind Star Wars, he always felt there were many more stories to tell. Through extensive interviews from 2016 to 2019, David brought those stories together for this book; The Galaxy Britain Built: The British Talent Behind Star Wars.

www.ingramcontent.com/pod-product-compliance
Lightning Source LLC
Chambersburg PA
CBHW050110170426
43198CB00014B/2528